Unbelievably Good Deals
& Great Adventures
That You
Absolutely Can't Get
Unless You're Over
50

Unbelievably Good Deals & Great Adventures That You Absolutely Can't Get Unless You're Over

50

JOAN RATTNER HEILMAN

CB
CONTEMPORARY
BOOKS
CHICAGO

Library of Congress Cataloging-in-Publication Data

Heilman, Joan Rattner.
   Unbelievably good deals and great adventures that
you absolutely can't get unless you're over 50.

   Includes index.
   1. Travel.   2. Discounts for the aged.   I. Title.
G151.H44   1988   910'.02   88-377
ISBN 0-8092-3926-4

Contents

Unbelievably Good Deals
& Great Adventures
That You
Absolutely Can't Get
Unless You're Over

50

Chapter One

Introduction to Good Deals and Great Adventures

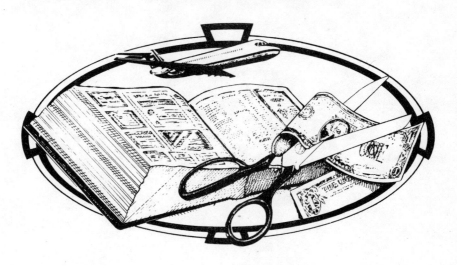

This book is for people who love to do interesting things and go to new places—and don't mind saving money while they're doing it. It is a guide to the perks, privileges, discounts, and special adventures to which you have become entitled simply because you've hung in there for 50 years or more.

On your 50th birthday (or on your 60th, 62nd, or 65th), you qualify for hundreds of special opportunities and money-saving offers that will have lots of people wishing they were older. All for a couple of good reasons. First, you deserve them, having successfully negotiated your way through life's white waters. And second, as the fastest-growing segment of the American population, you represent an enormous market of potential consumers, a fact that has become quite apparent to the business community. More than a quarter of the U.S. population today is over 50. One out of every eight Americans is over 65, outnumbering teenagers for the first time in history. Besides, life expectancy is higher today than ever before, and most of us can expect to live a long, healthy, and active life.

Those of us over 50 control most of the nation's wealth, including half of the discretionary income, the money that's left over after essentials have been taken care of, and 80 percent of the savings. For most of us, the children have gone, the mortgage has been paid off, the house is fully furnished, the goal of leaving a large inheritance is not a major concern, and the freedom years have arrived at last.

As a group, we're markedly different from previous older generations who pinched pennies and saved them all. We, too, know the value of a dollar, but we feel freer to spend our money because we're better off than our predecessors, a significant number of us having accumulated enough resources to be reasonably secure. We also are far better educated than those before us, and we have developed many more interests and activities.

And, most important, we as a group are remarkably fit, healthy, and energetic. We are in *very* good shape—and feel that way. In fact, a survey has shown that most of us feel at least 15 years younger than our chronological age.

The business community is actively courting "the mature market," as we are known, because now we have the time and the money to do all the things we've always put off. Because of the new recognition of our numbers, our flexible schedules, and our vast buying power, we are finally being taken very seriously. To get our attention, we are increasingly presented with some real breaks and good deals, all of which are detailed on these pages. We are also invited on trips and adventures specifically oriented toward our interests, needs, and abilities. You will find them here too.

In this book, you will learn how to get what's coming to you—the discounts and privileges you absolutely couldn't get if you were younger:

▶ The discounts at hotels and motels, at car-rental agencies, on buses, trains, and boats
▶ The best money-saving offers from the airlines that are eager for your patronage
▶ The colleges and universities that offer you an education for free—or nearly
▶ The insurance companies with discounts for people at 50 or thereabouts
▶ The trips, domestic and foreign, designed specifically for the mature market
▶ The free passes to all the national parks
▶ The ski resorts where you can ski for half price—or for nothing
▶ The tennis tournaments, road races, biking events, and senior softball leagues designed for you
▶ And much more!

Because every community has its own special perks to offer you, make a practice of *asking* if there are breaks to which you are entitled wherever you go, from movies to museums, concerts to historic sites, hotels to ski resorts, restaurants to riverboats, in this country and abroad. Don't expect clerks or ticket agents, tour operators, restaurant hosts, even travel agents to volunteer them to you. First, they may not think of it. Second, they may not realize you have reached the appropriate birthday. Third, they may not want to call attention to your age, just in case that's not something you would appreciate!

Remember to request your privileges *before* you pay or when you order or make reservations, and always carry proof of age or an over-50-club membership card, or, better yet, both. Sometimes the advantages come with membership, but often they are available to anyone over a specified age.

To make sure you're getting a legitimate discount when you want to take advantage of your over-50 privileges, call the hotel, airline, car-rental company, or tour operator and ask what the regular or normal prices are. Then decide whether you are getting a good deal. And, most important, always ask for *the lowest available rate* and compare that to your discounted rate. Frequently you'll find that even better specials are available to you.

With the help of this guidebook, you will have a wonderful time and save money too. Enjoy!

Chapter Two
Travel: Making Your Age Pay Off

People over 50 are the most ardent travelers of all. They travel more often, farther, more extravagantly, and for longer periods of time than anybody else. Ever since the travel industry discovered these facts, it's been after our business.

It's fallen in love with our age group because we have more discretionary income than people of other ages. And because we are wonderfully flexible. Many of us no longer have children in school, so we're free to travel at off-peak times or whenever we feel we need a change of scenery. In fact, we much prefer spring and fall to summer. Some of us have retired or have such good jobs that we can make our own schedules. We can even take advantage of midweek slack times when the industry is eager to fill space.

But, best of all, we are energetic, and we're not about to stay home too much. People over 50 account for about one-third of all domestic travel, air trips, hotel/motel nights, and trips to Europe and Africa. Nine out of ten of us are experienced travelers and savvy consumers.

Contrary to what a yuppie might think, people in the mature generation aren't content with watching the action; we like to get right into the middle of it. There's not a place we won't go or an activity we won't try. Though many of us prefer escorted tours, almost half of us choose to travel independently.

Not only that, but we're shrewd—we look for the best deals to the best places. We are experienced comparison shoppers and seek the most for our money.

For all these reasons, we are now offered astonishing numbers of travel-related discounts and reduced rates as well as special tour packages and other perks. Many agencies and tour operators have oriented all or part of their trips toward a mature clientele. Others include older travelers with everyone else but offer us special privileges.

Many of the airlines have formed travel "clubs" specifically for older travelers, giving discounts to members who pay a small membership fee to join, or offer coupon books, good for a year, that let us travel much more cheaply than other people. All of them give those of us over 62 at least a 10 percent reduction on fares. And most of the hotel and motel chains—as well as individual inns and hotels—now offer similar inducements, such as discounts on rooms and restaurants.

There are so many good deals and great adventures available to you when you are on the move that we'll start right off with travel.

But, first, keep in mind:

▶ Rates, trips, and privileges tend to change at a moment's notice, so check out each of them before you make your plans. Airlines and car-rental agencies are particularly capricious, and it's hard to tell what they offer from one week to the next. The good deals in this guidebook are those that are available as we go to press.

▶ Always ask for your discount when you make your reservations or at the time of purchase, order, or check-in. If you wait until you're checking out or settling your bill, it may be too late.

▶ Also remember that discounts may apply only between certain hours, on certain days of the week, or during specific seasons of the year. Check this out before making reservations and always remind the clerk of the discount when you check in or pay your fare.

▶ It's particularly important when traveling to carry identification with proof of age or membership in an over-50 organization such as AARP (see Chapter 19). In most cases, a driver's license or passport does the job. So, in some cases, does the organization's membership card, a birth certificate, a resident alien card, or any other official document showing your date of birth. If you're old enough for a Medicare card or Senior ID card, use that.

▶ Don't always spring for the senior discount without checking out other rates. Sometimes special promotional discounts available to anybody any age turn out to be better deals. The railroads, for example, are famous for this. Ask your travel agent or the ticket seller to figure out the *lowest possible available rate* for you at that moment.

▶ If you belong to an organization like AARP, some of these bargains are yours at age 50. Others come along a little later at varying birthdays, so watch for the cutoff points. Also, in many cases, if the person purchasing the ticket or trip is the right age, the rest of the party, a traveling companion, or the people sharing the room are entitled to the same reduced rates.

Chapter Three
Out-of-the-Ordinary Escapades

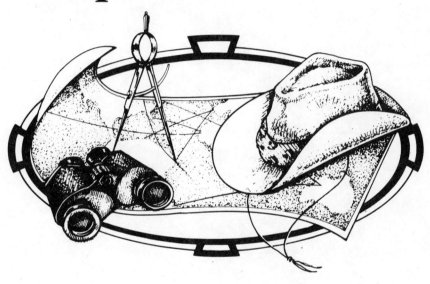

I f you are an intrepid, especially energetic, perhaps even courageous, sort of person who's intrigued by adventures that don't tempt the usual mature traveler, take a look at these possibilities. They are all designed to give you tales with which to regale your friends, relatives, and acquaintances—at least until you embark on the next one!

ALASKA WILDLAND ADVENTURES

For close encounters with wildlife and views of spectacular scenery, sign up for a Senior Safari offered by Alaska Wildland Adventures, a company that specializes in "soft adventure." You'll meet in Anchorage for an eight-day trip, led by a trained naturalist, that starts off with an outdoor salmon bake and includes wildlife tours by van through national parks and refuges, visits to historic bush towns, a cruise aboard a yacht, whale watching, scenic drives, and overnights in comfortable lodges. The 14 senior departures a year are limited to 18 people and all take place in the summer months, with the first and last nights spent at a hotel in Anchorage. Grandchildren are welcome to go along with you. If you belong to any senior organization, you will get a $50 discount per person. Just ask for it.

For information: Alaska Wildland Adventures, PO Box 259, Trout Lake, WA 98650; 1-800-334-8730.

AMERICAN WILDERNESS EXPERIENCE

If you love adventure travel and enjoy roughing it, consider the trips from AWE, which offers its own trips as well as those of many tour operators in the West. Although all of the travel is open to all ages, people over 65 get a 5 to 10 percent discount on some. For example, several of the horseback pack trips through wilderness areas offer slightly reduced senior rates, as do some of the adventures that combine activities (for example, a six-day trip that includes riding, rock climbing, biking, and rafting; another that combines riding and rafting). **For information:** American Wilderness Experience, PO Box 1486, Boulder, CO 80306; 1-800-444-0099 or 303-494-2992.

AMERICAN YOUTH HOSTELS

The outfit that sends teenagers on low-cost bike trips all over the world is not for youth alone. In fact, it offers an array of inexpensive adventures—bike tours and otherwise—specifically to people over 50. And, of course, older people are invited to go along on any AYH trips labeled "for adults." A recent cycling trip to New Zealand, for example, was composed of bikers ranging in age from 23 to 70.

If you want to go on an AYH Discovery Tour, you must become a member. Membership for adults is $25 a year, unless you've reached 55, in which case you pay only $15. Members get a card and a guidebook that lists hostels in the United States and Canada. You may purchase handbooks for Europe and other areas of the world.

The United States affiliate of the International Youth Hostel Federation that coordinates more than 5,300 hostels in 61 countries, AYH has been operating for over half a century. Each of its trips is limited to 10 participants, including the trip leader. You'll stay primarily in hostels, which are inexpensive dormitory-style accommodations, no two of them alike. You might stay in a castle in Germany or a lighthouse in California or a budget motel in Massachusetts. Most hostels have kitchens where your group prepares its own meals, although a few have cafeterias.

Each year, AYH plans several itineraries for the over-50 crowd, often including backpacking or cycling tours, hiking tours by van with day hikes, and train trips. The recent roster offered van/hiking trips through northern New Mexico or to the mountains and lakes of Alaska, cycling in New England, and two weeks in the national parks of the Southwest.

In addition to all that, you are entitled to lodge at any hostel in the world, including the new network of urban hostels now in Chicago; Washington, D.C.; New York; Boston; San Francisco; Miami Beach; New Orleans; and Los Angeles (one night's stay costs $5 to $20). There is no maximum age limitation for booking a bed in these wonderfully cheap lodgings and hobnobbing with other hostelers who prefer not to pay exorbitant hotel prices. Be ready, however, to sleep in a double-decker cot in a sex-segregated dormitory for about six or eight people supervised by "hostel parents."

For information: American Youth Hostels, Dept. 855, PO Box 37613, Washington, DC 20013-7613; 202-783-6161.

CANADIAN HOSTELLING ASSOCIATION
Canada's hostelling program is similar to that of AYH, although it does not offer adventures designed exclusively for people over 50. Instead, it invites you to join any of its adult trips (here, too, there is no maximum age limit), and hosts Elderhostel Canada programs at some of its more than 70 properties. In addition, as a member, you may lodge at a hostel for $6 to $20 per night, with meals from $2, in Canada—or at any other hostel in the world. Membership for one year costs $25.
For information: Canadian Hostelling Association (L'Association Canadienne de l'Ajisme), 1600 James Naismith Dr., Ste. 608, Gloucester, Ontario, Canada K1B 5N4; 613-748-5638.

CREATIVE ADVENTURE CLUB
This agency offers 15-day soft adventures to South America and the Asia-Pacific area, including Thailand, Borneo, Malaysia, Nepal, Australia, and New Guinea. The exotic trips are designed to go at a pace that's relaxed enough to suit most mature travelers and often include activities such as snorkeling, hiking, mountain trekking, caving, and train tours as well as basic sightseeing. Some of the tours are specifically for seniors, while others include all ages.
For information: Creative Adventure Club, 3007 Royce Lane, Costa Mesa, CA 92626; 800-544-5088.

MT. ROBSON ADVENTURE HOLIDAYS

For people who love participatory trips, this outfit plans a couple of adventure vacations every year strictly for people over 50. All of the trips are in Yoho National Park or Mount Robson Provincial Park, home of the highest mountain in the Canadian Rockies. Golden Week includes two days of hiking, one or two days of canoeing on spectacular mountain lakes, and a one-day historical tour. You sleep in heated log cabins at the base camp. Or you may choose a five-day heli-camping trip. You are taken by helicopter to a tent camp on the shores of a lake, where you take day trips to points affording spectacular views.

For information: Mt. Robson Adventure Holidays, PO Box 146, Valemount, BC V0E 2Z0, Canada; 604-566-4351 or 604-566-4386.

OUTWARD BOUND USA

Known for its wilderness-survival trips for youngsters and young adults so they can gain self-confidence and self-esteem and learn to work as a team, Outward Bound has short and popular courses specifically for those at least 50 or sometimes 55. The physical activities are less strenuous than they are for 16-year-olds, but you are expected to push yourself and the goal is the same—to help you discover that there are self-imposed limits, physical and mental, that you can go beyond. Some of the courses have the special goal of helping to effect a smooth transition from career to retirement.

The special four- to nine-day courses for people over 50 include canoeing in the Everglades and whitewater rafting in the Green River in Utah.

On Outward Bound trips, you live in a tent or under a tarp, sleep in a sleeping bag, cook your own food. You must be in good health although you need not be a veteran athlete.

For information: Outward Bound USA, 384 Field Point Rd., Greenwich, CT 06830; 1-800-243-8520 (in Connecticut, 203-661-0797).

GOOD DEAL FOR RVers

International Camper Exchange puts you in touch, at no charge, with people in other countries (notably the UK) who are interested in swapping RVs for a certain period of time, not necessarily simultaneously. When you exchange rigs, you've got a bargain vacation, because no money changes hands and you'll travel rent-free. It takes time to arrange the swap, so sign up many months or even a year before you'd like to travel. You'll receive the names and addresses of one or more interested families, if available, and you take it from there, making your own arrangements.

For information: Send a stamped, self-addressed envelope to International Camper Exchange, 14226 442nd Ave. SE, North Bend, WA 98045.

THE OVER THE HILL GANG

The Gang is a club that welcomes fun-loving, adventurous, peppy people over 50 who are looking for action and contemporaries to pursue it with. No naps, no rockers, no sitting by the pool sipping planter's punch. The Over the Hill Gang started as a ski club many years ago but now is into lots of different activities, including travel (see Chapters 13 and 14 for more about the club). Most of the trips are sports-oriented, but some are just plain trips. For example, recent choices have included ski trips to Keystone, Copper Mountain, Breckenridge, Vail, and other ski areas in the West; New Zealand; the Alps; and the Arlberg of Austria. Other recent trips: whitewater rafting on the Colorado and Rogue rivers; and travel in Scandinavia and the Soviet Union.

Join the national organization for $37 ($60 per couple) and, if there is a chapter in your area, you may join it too for small additional yearly dues. You'll never lack for company and interesting places to go.

For information: Over the Hill Gang International, 6635 S. Dayton St., Ste. 220, Englewood, CO 80111; 303-790-2724.

GOING WITH THE GRANDCHILDREN

GRANDTRAVEL

GrandTravel is an innovative vacation program that offers trips for grandparents and their grandchildren so they can share the pleasures of traveling together. "It's a great way to strengthen the link between generations and create lasting memories for everyone," says Helena Koenig, the travel agent who started it. GrandTravel's series of itineraries, scheduled for normal school breaks, aims to appeal to both generations. It includes summer tours to England; trips to Washington, D.C., or Alaska; tours through the American Southwest, northern California, or Maine; a cruise of the Hawaiian islands; African safaris; a visit to Australia; a tour of western national parks; and barge trips in Holland. GrandTravel will also arrange for independent grandparent/grandchild travel, family groups, or school-sponsored groups.

Actually, you don't have to be a grandparent to take the trips—aunts, uncles, cousins, godparents, and other surrogate grannies are welcome. Ranging from 7 to 18 days, the tours, led by teacher-escorts, include good hotels with recreation facilities, transportation by motorcoach with rest stops every two hours, games, talks, music on the buses, and a travel manual for every tour. Each trip includes time for the older folks and the children to be alone with their own age group. The kids may go roller skating and dine on fried chicken—supervised, of course—while the grandparents do something grown up, such as going to a gourmet restaurant for dinner.
For information: GrandTravel, The Ticket Counter, 6900 Wisconsin Ave., Chevy Chase, MD 20815; 1-800-247-7651 (in Maryland, 301-986-0790).

GRANDPARENT/GRANDCHILDREN HOLIDAYS
Saga Holidays offers another way for two generations to explore the world together. Its Grandparents Program lets you invite a grandchild along at a reduced rate on some departures for both land tours and cruises. See Chapter 7 for more about Saga's offerings.
For information: Saga Holidays, 120 Boylston St., Boston, MA 02116; 1-800-343-0273.

R.F.D. TRAVEL
Find new traveling companions: go with your grandkids! With special attractions scheduled along the way for the

young folks, this tour operator has put together a couple of trips for the two generations for summer vacation times. The itineraries may vary each year, but recent grandparent/grandchildren adventures have included an American Heritage tour encompassing Washington, D.C., Gettysburg, Philadelphia, Williamsburg, and Richmond and a mid-Atlantic fall foliage tour. Plans are underway for Alaska as well as the Rose Bowl.

For information: R.F.D. Travel, 5201 Johnson Dr., Mission, KS 66205; 1-800-365-5359.

VISTATOURS
The GrandVista tours for grandparents and grandchildren available from Vistatours are designed to make everybody happy with a wide choice of one-week trips to such places as a Texas ranch, Mt. Rushmore and the Badlands of South Dakota, the sights around Reno and Tahoe, and a tour of New England. The plans include activities for the two generations separately and together, and the goal is for grandparents and grandchildren to become closer through shared experiences.

For information: Vistatours, 1923 N. Carson St., Ste. 105, Carson City, NV 89701; 1-800-647-0800.

GRANDPARENTS CAMP
See pages 200–201 for details about a week in the country with your grandchildren during the summer.

GRANDPEOPLE TOURS
Here's a way to spend some magic time together with your grandchild while you travel to places of special interest to both of you. The intergenerational Grand-

People Tours run by Schilling Travel are designed specifically for the two age groups, with lots of activities and plenty of free time to get to know the "Grand-Group." Current destinations scheduled during school vacations with more coming along later include a journey through Vermont, an exploration of the Fairy-Tale Road in Germany, and a tour of the Soviet Union.

For information: GrandPeople Tours, Schilling Travel, 722 Second Avenue South, Minneapolis, MN 55402; 1-800-992-1903.

Chapter Four
Cutting Your Costs Abroad

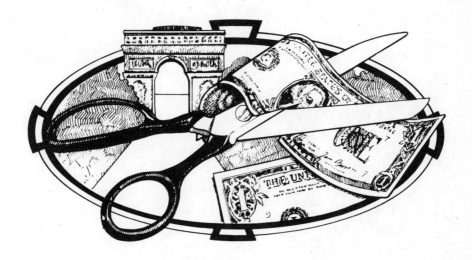

The most enthusiastic voyagers of all age groups, Americans over 50—one out of three adults and a quarter of the total population—spend more time and money on travel than anybody else, especially when it comes to going abroad. It's been estimated that more than 4 out of every 10 passport holders are at least 55 years old. And there's hardly a country in the world today that doesn't actively encourage mature travelers to come for a visit, because everybody has discovered that you are travel's "Now Generation."

Because you are currently being hotly pursued, you can take advantage of many good deals in other lands. This chapter gives you a rundown on ways to cut your European holiday costs, especially if you are planning your trip on your own.

But, first, keep in mind:

▶ Because this is a rapidly changing field as more and more nations and tourist attractions jump on the senior bandwagon, always check the rates as you go. You may find new bargains.
▶ Always have your necessary identification with you (your passport is an excellent ID) and don't be afraid to ask if your age qualifies you for a discount or special fare.

EUROPE BY RAIL

EURAILPASS

To begin with, there is the well-known Eurailpass, valid for unlimited first-class train travel in 17 European countries (including Ireland but not Great Britain). There is no senior discount, but it's certainly worth buying if you plan to cover a lot of miles. Available for various numbers of days up to three months, the passes also get you free or reduced rates on many buses, ferries, and steamers. Traveling with a group of three or more people (or two or more in the off-season) and thereby qualifying for a Eurail Saverpass is especially cheap.

You must buy your Eurailpass before leaving home.
For information: Call your travel agent or write to Eurailpass, Box 325, Old Greenwich, CT 06870.

COUNTRY-BY-COUNTRY TRAVEL DEALS

AUSTRIA

Travel half price anywhere in Austria on the Austrian Federal Railways and its buses by using a Railway Senior Citizen's ID Card. You must be 60 if you are a woman, or 65 if you are a man, to be entitled to purchase the card at major railroad stations and some post offices in the country. Take proof of your age (your passport) and an extra passport-size photo. The card is good for a year and currently costs approximately $20. It is not available in the U.S., but you may send for it by mail.
For information: Austrian National Tourist Office, 500 Fifth Ave., New York, NY 10036; 212-944-6880.

BERMUDA

February is Golden Rendezvous Month in Bermuda, it's a time when special activities, entertainment, and discounts are available to you if you are over 50. Hotels offer special travel packages and golf courses run over-50 tournaments. You'll attend interesting lectures on such subjects as Bermuda culture, architecture, and flora and fauna and will be entitled to tours of the island. Go to the Visitors Service Bureau on Front Street in Hamilton to pick up free ferry and bus tokens plus a coupon book offering discounts at stores and sight-seeing attractions.

For information: Call 1-800-223-6106 (in New York, 1-800-223-6107).

FRANCE

The Carte Vermeil for anyone over 60 entitles you to purchase rail tickets within France for half price in either first or second class. Currently selling for 165 French francs at major railroad stations in France, it is good for a year and makes a lot of sense if you are planning an extended stay and considerable moving about. Usually, the 50 percent reduction applies from noon on Saturday until 3 P.M. on Sunday and from noon on Monday until noon on Friday. It is not valid on certain blackout days.

If you plan to travel extensively around Europe, you can purchase a Carte Rail Europ Senior card in addition to the Carte Vermeil. It costs an additional 55 francs at this writing and allows you to travel, with restrictions, in 19 countries. It, too, is available at major railroad stations in France.

In addition, for half price on some domestic air travel,

at movies, museums, and other cultural activities, anyone French or foreign who is 65 must only show proof of age.
For information: Rail Europe, 226–230 Westchester Ave., White Plains, NY 10604; 1-800-345-1990.

GERMANY

Germanrail's Senioren-Pass offered to everyone over 60 is good for a 50 percent reduction on regular fares in first and second class. It's also valid on some railroads in other countries if you start and finish your trip in Germany. Two varieties are available. Pass A is good only on Mondays, Tuesdays, Wednesdays, Thursdays, and Saturdays. Pass B, a little more expensive, will do the job every day of the week. Both are valid for a year. Purchase your pass at any major railroad station, using your passport as proof of age. Take along an extra passport-size photograph for the card.
For information: Germanrail, 747 Third Ave., New York, NY 10017; 212-308-3100.

GREAT BRITAIN

Here's where you're going to get some of the best bargains in Europe, because the British are really into "the very good years," by which they usually mean over 60. There are discounts and special rates on just about everything—railroads, airlines, hotels, museums, day cruises, theaters, and historical and tourist sites.

The BritRail Senior Pass and the Senior Flexipass (for travelers 60 and over) give you reduced rates for consecutive days on 8-day, 15-day, 22-day, or one-month passes, first class or standard, for unlimited travel in

England, Scotland, and Wales. The rates are even better than with the regular BritRail Pass, which is a bargain for everyone else. The Senior Flexipass is the same idea but allows unlimited rail travel on 4 out of 8 days, 8 out of 15 days, or 15 days out of one month. The pass must be purchased through your travel agent *before* you leave this continent—it is not sold in Britain. By the way, the Eurailpass is not accepted in Great Britain.

In Northern Ireland, you may wish to avail yourself of a Rail Runabout ticket that gives you seven days of unlimited travel on all scheduled rail services at half price. You must be 65 for this privilege. The Freedom of Northern Ireland tickets do the same on all scheduled bus services except coach tours. Choose a one-day or a seven-day ticket.

People of other ages need the Britexpress Card for one-third off the fare throughout England, Scotland, and Wales on express buses operated by the National Express Bus Company and Scottish Citylink Coaches— but you don't. That's because you automatically get a one-third reduction on any bus fare simply by showing proof of your age.

Be sure to buy a Great British Heritage Pass—again before you leave home. It gets you free admission to more than 600 castles, palaces, and stately homes and gardens in the British Isles, including the Tower of London and Windsor Castle.

If you're going to spend much time in London, buy the London Visitor Travelcard through your travel agent, again before you go. With it, you will get unlimited rides on the city's bus and underground systems as well as tube travel to and from Heathrow Airport for three, four, or seven consecutive days.

Most theaters offer senior discounts, although sometimes only for matinees. Check at the box office or ask the hotel concierge.

Hotels also often give senior discounts in the off-season (November through March), so always inquire when you make your reservations. The most notable are the Scottish Highland Hotels, whose Golden Times rates are 20 percent less all year for anybody over 60.

For information: The British Tourist Authority, 40 W. 57th St., New York, NY 10019; 212-581-4700. For rail passes: BritRail, 1500 Broadway, New York, NY 10036; 1-800-677-8585 (in New York state, 212-575-2667).

MAKING FRIENDS BY MAIL

International Pen Friends is a pen-pal organization with members all over the world. Anybody any age is eligible to join (the membership fee is slightly less if you're over 60) and be matched up with pen friends in other countries—an excellent way to make interesting contacts or practice a foreign language and to have friends to visit when you travel. You receive a list of 14 names of people who are in your age group and share your interests, in a choice of countries and/or languages. There are now about 300,000 IPF members in 156 countries.

For information: Send a self-addressed, stamped envelope to International Pen Friends, PO Box 65, Homecrest Station, Brooklyn, NY 11229; 718-769-1785.

Golden Pen-Pal Association of North America is another way to broaden your horizons. It will match you up with a compatible correspondent in another part of the United States.

For information: Send a self-addressed, stamped envelope to Golden Pen-Pal Association of North America, 1304 Hedgelawn Way, Raleigh, NC 27615.

GREECE
Here, if you are 60, male or female, you may buy a Hellenic Railways pass that's good for five free single train trips within Greece. When you've used up your five trips, you may travel on trains and buses at a 50 percent reduction. Valid for one year, the pass may be purchased at any major railroad station in Greece. The only hitch: there are some blackout periods when the card doesn't do the trick. These, of course, probably fall just when you don't want them to—from July 1 to the end of September, plus the 10 days before and after Easter and Christmas.
For information: The Greek National Tourist Organization, 645 Fifth Ave., New York, NY 10022; 212-421-5777.

ITALY
The Carta d'Argento (Silver Card), which costs a few dollars and is valid for a year, entitles everyone age 60, tourist or resident, to a 30 percent discount on Italian railways. It can be purchased at railroad stations in Italy at the special windows (Biglietti Speciali) and at C.I.T. offices. Later, flash the card when you buy your tickets. Note that if you are planning extensive train travel in Italy, however, you may wish to buy a travel-anywhere pass (available to tourists of all ages). Called BLTC, it is valid for unlimited travel for 8, 15, 21, or 30 days. It's cheap and may be a better buy for you. It may be purchased in the United States or in Italy.
For information: Get a BLTC through your travel agent or from Italian State Railways, 594 Broadway, New York, NY 10012; 212-274-0593.

LUXEMBOURG

Anybody over 65 pays half fare on trains and buses. Ask for the discount when you buy your tickets.

For information: The Luxembourg National Tourist Office, 801 Second Ave., New York, NY 10017; 212-370-9850.

THE NETHERLANDS

For rail travel in the Netherlands, you may wish to buy a Senior Pass if you are 60 or more and plan to spend a lot of time in this charming country. Available at railroad stations, the pass is valid for one year and entitles you to 40 percent off the regular fares on one-way tickets, first or second class, after 9 A.M. Monday through Friday most of the year. On weekends and during the months of July and August, it gets you the discount at any hour. At this writing, the pass costs approximately $40.

The Holland Leisure Card, available to all ages, is also worth considering. For a few dollars, it gives you discounts on hotels, car rentals, trains, domestic air travel, and tourist attractions. The Holland Leisure Card Plus provides the same benefits plus the Museum card, which gives you free admission to over 300 museums. It's best to buy the card in the U.S. before you go, but you may buy it at any tourist office in the Netherlands.

For information: The Netherlands Board of Tourism, 355 Lexington Ave., New York, NY 10017; 212-370-7367.

PORTUGAL

When you travel in Portugal, you may acquire a Gold Card at any major railroad station simply by displaying your passport to prove that you are over 60. The Gold

Card gives you a 50 percent discount on rail travel within Portugal. The only restriction on its use is on suburban lines during rush hours: 6:30 to 9:30 A.M. and 4 to 8 P.M. Monday through Friday.

For information: Portuguese National Tourist Office, 590 Fifth Ave., New York, NY 10036; 212-354-4403.

SCANDINAVIAN COUNTRIES

If you are a senior over 65, you can travel in the four Scandinavian countries—Denmark, Sweden, Norway, and Finland—more cheaply than other people can.

Denmark: You can buy train tickets for half fare except during peak hours (Friday, 2 P.M. to 7 P.M.; Saturday, 8 A.M. to noon; Sunday, 2 P.M. to midnight) and major holiday periods. Simply show proof of your age when you buy your tickets.

Sweden: The Swedish State Railways (SJ) give a 30 percent markdown, with no restrictions on days or times. The discount also applies on the company's bus routes. Boats and ferries, too, offer special senior fares which vary according to the season. Again, be prepared to prove your age when you buy tickets.

Norway: Norway's offer is half price for a train ticket, first or second class, any time, anywhere. To get this, however, you or your spouse must be 67.

Finland: The Senior Citizen card, available for a few Finn marks at railroad or bus stations, entitles you to half fare on trains and 30 percent off on bus trips that are at least 75 kilometers one way.

Also look into the Scandinavian Bonus Pass. It is not age-oriented but gives discounts off the rates at more than a hundred first-class hotels during the summer season.

And consider picking up a city card—Copenhagen Card, Oslo Card, Helsinki Card, Stockholm Card—at tourist offices, airports, or hotels in the capital cities; cards are also available for Tampere, Finland, and Gothenburg and Malmo, Sweden. The cards, which cost only a small amount of money, simplify your life in these cities by giving you unlimited travel on city transportation, free entry to museums and attractions, and discounts on sight-seeing tours, hotels, car rentals, restaurants, guided walking tours, and events.

For information: The Scandinavian National Tourist Offices, 655 Third Ave., New York, NY 10017; 212-949-2333.

SWITZERLAND

Switzerland offers some of the best discounts around. As part of its Season for Seniors, the Swiss Hotel Association will provide, for the asking, a list of over 450 hotels that give reduced rates to women over 62 and men over 65 (if you are a couple, only one of you must be the required minimum age). The only catch is that in most cases the discounted rates are not offered during peak seasons, including the summer months.

Although the following travel passes are not just for mature travelers but are available to everyone, they are worth noting because they may save you considerable money on fares. The first is the Swiss Pass, useful if you are planning to do extensive traveling within the country because it allows you unlimited trips on the Swiss Travel System, including most private and mountain railroads, lake steamers, and most postal motorcoaches, public tramways, and buses in 25 cities. It also lets you buy excursion tickets to mountaintops at 25 percent off. Buy it for eight days, 15 days, or one month.

The second is the cheaper Swiss Half-Fare Card, available only in Switzerland, with one version that's valid for a year and another for a month. Using the card, you may buy half-price tickets on the national travel lines.

And the third is the Swiss Card. Valid for one month, it gives you one free trip from any entry point to your destination within Switzerland and return. In addition, with the Card you may purchase an unlimited number of tickets on all scheduled services by train, postal coach, or lake steamer at half price.

For information: Swiss National Tourist Office, 608 Fifth Ave., New York, NY 10020; 212-757-5944. In Switzerland, the transport cards are available at railroad stations and airports.

Chapter Five
Trips and Tours for the Mature Traveler

A few sagacious over-50 organizations and travel agencies now cater to "the mature traveler." They choose destinations sure to appeal to those who have already seen much of the world, arrange trips that are leisurely and unhassled, give you like-minded contemporaries to travel with plus group hosts to smooth the way, and provide many services you've decided you're now entitled to. They also give you a choice between strenuous action-filled tours and those that are more relaxed. In fact, most of the agencies offer so many choices that the major problem becomes making a decision about where to go.

Options range from cruises in the Caribbean or the Greek Isles to grand tours of the Orient, sight-seeing excursions in the United States, trips to the Canadian Rockies, theater tours of London, African safaris and snorkeling vacations on the Great Barrier Reef off Australia. There's no place in the world over-50s won't go.

Among the newer and most popular trends are apartment-hotel complexes in American and European resort areas, as well as apartments in major cities. Here you can stay put for as long as you like, using the apartment as a home base for short-range roaming and exploring.

To qualify for most of the trips, one member of the party is supposed to meet the minimum age requirement, and the rest may be younger.

RETIRING IN THE SUNBELT

National Retirement Concepts specializes in helping you find an ideal place to retire in the U.S. It organizes small, reasonably priced one-week group tours, for singles and couples, to six Sunbelt retirement areas—Arizona, Arkansas, North and South Carolina, and the two coasts of Florida—to help you scout a likely spot to settle down. Escorted, you combine a sight-seeing vacation with visits to retirement communities and conversations with the locals. The idea is that it is much easier to make a relocation decision after you've done your own investigating.

For information: National Retirement Concepts, 1454 N. Wieland Ct., Chicago, IL 60610; 1-800-888-2312 (in Illinois, 312-951-2866).

THE OVER-50 CLUBS

AARP TRAVEL EXPERIENCE

AARP (see Chapter 19) is a huge club that offers all kinds of wonderful benefits to its 50-plus members, including dozens of group land/air tours and cruises, all planned by American Express with mature voyagers in mind. To sign on with a trip, you now have three options: call toll-free, visit an American Express travel office, or use your own travel agent.

Constantly updated by mailings informing you of new offerings, you'll choose from a vast selection of group travel programs, all escorted by tour managers or hosts. The list of choices is enormous, with motorcoach tours fron Europe to China and Alaska to Brazil, cruises all over the world, and vacations within the United States and Canada that include tours of the Old South and of fishing villages in Nova Scotia as well as rafting trips down the Colorado.

If group travel isn't your bag, however, and you prefer to go on your own, you may decide to spend a week or more in your own apartment or hotel, perhaps in Europe or Costa Rica or Hawaii, on a Hosted Visit, with a local AARP host on hand for advice and assistance. Or pick a fly/drive tour in the U.S. or Europe, complete with planned itineraries and prearranged overnight lodgings.

For information: AARP Travel Experience from American Express; for land tours: 1-800-927-0111; for cruises: 1-800-745-4567.

TRAVELING FOR LESS

Senior travelers—in this case, those over 55—can join the **SecondWind Travel Club** and get discounts of 10 to 50 percent at attractions, restaurants, and hotels especially in the Western states, with the promise that the discounts are better than the usual senior discounts. SecondWind also offers discounts off the already-special fares or the applicable senior citizen fares on airline tickets. Introduced by the nonprofit Senior Travel & Recreation Activities Council (STRAC), SecondWind Travel Club gives members a discount card, a travel directory, a quarterly newsletter, and a toll-free number for information on destinations and airline bookings. At this writing, the membership fee is $8 a year at age 55 (plus $5 a year for a spouse).

For information: STRAC SecondWind Travel Club, PO Box 1142, Redondo Beach, CA 90278; 213-370-5094.

TRAVEL AGENCIES THAT CATER TO OVER-50s

SAGA HOLIDAYS

Founded decades ago in England, Saga is now the largest company in the world that specializes in travel for people in their prime. On its trips, which may be booked only by direct mail or telephone and not through travel agents, it accepts travelers over 60 (and their spouses or friends over 50). Once your name is on Saga's mailing list, you will be faced with constant temptation because the enticing brochures keep on coming.

This agency offers a wide variety of vacations, from fully escorted coach tours everywhere in the world to cruises and safaris, educational tours, and winter apartment stays. You may travel with a group or on your own. Cruises include trips along the coastline of Alaska, through the Panama Canal, down the Mississippi, expeditions to Antarctica, and barge trips in France. To let you live a while in one place, Saga provides Extended Stay Holidays—in Portugal, Spain, Florida, Arizona, and London, for example—where you'll live in your own furnished apartment or hotel for as long as you choose.

More Saga programs: In partnership with the Smithsonian Institution, the agency offers the Smithsonian Odyssey Tours, where you explore the world and learn as you go, led by knowledgeable study leaders. Its Garden Tours take you to some of the great gardens of the world, this time escorted by a garden specialist. If you like to travel on your own, you may have your trip arranged by Saga's Independent Travel program, or if you prefer out-of-the-way places, you may choose a Backroads of Europe adventure.

And there's more: a Grandparents Program that lets you take a grandchild along at a reduced rate on some tours, and World Club Jamborees, which are gatherings of Saga travelers getting together in exotic settings.
For information: Saga Holidays, 120 Boylston St., Boston, MA 02116; 1-800-343-0273, 9:00 A.M. to 5:30 P.M. EST.

GRAND CIRCLE TRAVEL

Grand Circle caters to people over 50 and plans all of its trips specifically for them. Founded 34 years ago, this tour operator was the first U.S. company to market senior travel and has escorted more than 600,000 Americans all over the world.

Grand Circle specializes in "Extended Vacations." On these trips, you live in an apartment or residential hotel that serves as your home base—in such places as Mexico, England, Spain, Portugal, Switzerland, Costa Rica, and Turkey—for two to 26 weeks. Staying put for a while gives you plenty of time to explore at your leisure.

In addition, GCT also offers traditional escorted international and domestic tours as well as cruises.

As for single travelers, it gives a 50 percent discount on the standard hotel and apartment single supplements if you have requested a travel roommate and none is available for your trip. And on a few departure dates for Extended Vacations there is no single supplement charge at all.
For information: Grand Circle Travel, 347 Congress St., Boston, MA 02210; 1-800-248-3737 Monday through Friday 8:00 A.M. to 7:00 P.M. EST and Saturday 9:00 A.M. to 5:00 P.M. EST.

GOLDEN AGE TRAVELLERS

This over-50 club specializes in discounted cruises to just about everywhere in the world but offers land trips as well. When you join the club ($10 a year or $15 per couple), you will receive a quarterly newsletter with listings of upcoming adventures, discounts, and bonuses on major cruise lines. Other inducements are tour escorts on every venture and credits against the transportation costs to the airport on certain trips. Single travelers may choose to be enrolled in the "Roommates Wanted" list to help them find a companion to share the cabin and the costs.

For members in the San Francisco and Sacramento areas, there are one-day minitours and meetings where you may meet fellow travelers. Especially intriguing to mature travelers are this agency's long-stay trips. On these, you stay put—in such places as Spain or Portugal, Costa Rica or Argentina—at the same hotel for two or three weeks, and, if you wish, take short side excursions. The packages include air, hotel, and sometimes meals.
For information: Golden Age Travellers, Pier 27, the Embarcadero, San Francisco, CA 94111; 1-800-258-8880 (in California, 1-800-652-1683).

AJS TRAVEL CONSULTANTS, INC.

The 50 Plus Club, which packages tours for older travelers, is the special concern of AJS Travel Consultants. It markets a series of discounted tours, all leisurely and escorted, ranging from 11 days to 22. Specialties include Switzerland and Czechoslovakia and especially Israel, where many eventful but relaxed tours are scheduled throughout the year.

For information: AJC Travel Consultants, 177 Beach & 116th St., Rockaway Park, NY 11694; 1-800-221-5002 or 718-945-5900.

MORE, MORE, MORE

ADRIATIC TOURS
All-inclusive senior tours are a specialty of Adriatic Tours, an agency that sends you on off-season (October to April) low-cost holidays in several Mediterranean countries. Most trips are for two weeks, but you may stay longer at very little cost per week or add mini-vacations to Athens, Budapest, Istanbul, or Rome. Added features: dances, lectures, health spas.
For information: Call your travel agent or contact Adriatic Tours, 691 W. 10th St., San Pedro, CA 90731; 1-800-262-1718.

BACK-ROAD TOURING CO.
Designed especially for adults over 50, the tours planned by this agency take small groups (no more than 12 at a time) through the British Isles, Ireland, and France along the back roads to out-of-the-way places. You travel with a guide for one or two weeks by minivan, stay in inns, historic houses, farms, and bed-and-breakfasts, and don't spend a fortune. If you organize your own group of eight travelers, you and a companion get to travel free. These are leisurely tours with plenty of time to explore. You may even help plan the itinerary if there are special places you'd like to see. Add-on stays in London are available too. What's more, if you mention this book you will get a discount.

For information: Back-Road Touring Co., c/o Chusa, Inc., 242 Bellevue Ave., Upper Montclair, NJ 07043; 1-800-526-2915 (in New Jersey, 201-744-8724).

BONANZA HOLIDAYS

The winter long-stay holidays offered by Bonanza's Club 50 from mid-January through March take you, inexpensively, via Air Canada to such places as Spain's Costa del Sol, Portugal's Algarve, Tunisia, Hawaii, Egypt, southern California, or Turkey. There you settle in for three weeks or so, taking side trips as you like. All departures are from Toronto, with nominal add-on fares for those from other locations. Most overseas holidays include a few nights in London.

For information: Call your travel agent or contact Bonanza Holidays, 310 N. Queen St., Suite 201 N., Etobicoke, ON M9C 5K4, Canada.

CANNON TOURS & TRAVEL

The 50's Plus program of Cannon Tours, a Canadian tour operator headquartered in Toronto, specializes in three categories of inexpensive holidays for the older crowd. Its "Go-Go" tours are designed for energetic folks who can tolerate long flights and full sight-seeing days (for example, tours of the Soviet Union and the South Pacific). "Slow-Go" trips, perhaps to the Canadian West and the Rockies, or California and Arizona, spend a few nights in each place and limit the length of the driving from hither to yon. "No-Go" are stays all in one place, such as St. Petersburg, Scottsdale, or Victoria, British Columbia.

For information: Call your travel agent or contact Cannon Tours & Travel, 234 Eglinton Ave. East, Toronto, ON M4P 1K5, Canada; 416-481-6177.

CHOOSING A PLACE TO RETIRE
Lifestyle Explorations conducts two-week group tours in countries that it considers to be ideal retirement destinations. You may choose tours of Costa Rica, Portugal, Uruguay and Argentina, Honduras, or Ireland, combining a vacation with on-site seminars with local professionals and Americans already living there. You'll discover firsthand what it's like to settle there before you make any big decisions. Each area is rated according to cost of living, taxes, health care, climate, safety, friendliness, government stability, and cultural opportunities.
For information: Lifestyle Explorations, World Trade Center, Suite 400, Boston, MA 02210; 508-371-4814.

FOLKWAYS INSTITUTE
This institute offers educational, cultural, and natural-history workshops and study tours in exotic places and currently lists about a dozen Senior Studies programs specifically for people age 55 and over. The programs are designed to heighten cultural awareness in such parts of the world as China, Kenya, Tibet, India, Peru, Greece, and Europe, and several provide close looks at the native cuisine. Groups are limited to 16 and are accompanied by knowledgeable guides.
For information: Folkways Institute, 14600 Southeast Aldridge Rd., Portland, OR 97236; 1-800-225-4666.

LOVE HOLIDAYS
For the "mature sophisticated traveler," Love Holidays features trips to Eastern Europe—Austria, Hungary, Greece, Poland, Czechoslovakia, Bulgaria, Romania, Turkey, and the Soviet Union. Its all-inclusive packages are escorted.

For information: Call your travel agent or contact Love Holidays, 15315 Magnolia Blvd., Sherman Oaks, CA 91403; 1-800-456-5683 (in the Los Angeles area, 213-873-7991).

MAYFLOWER TOURS

Mayflower plans trips for people "55 or better." Most departures are from Chicago with overnight accommodations arranged for travelers from surrounding states. Some of the agency's more far-flung tours, however, leave from other cities. All trips are fully escorted by tour directors whose job it is to make sure all goes well and everybody has fun. The pace is leisurely, and rest stops are scheduled for every couple of hours. You travel by air-conditioned motorcoach, stay in quality hotels or motels, and eat most of your meals together.

If you are a single traveler and make your trip reservation at least 45 days before departure, you'll get a roommate or travel at the regular two-to-a-room tour cost.

Most of the agency's trips are within the United States (Hawaii included), with tours, for example, through the Canadian Rockies, Alaska, the Southwest, Florida, Georgia, New England, and New York.

For information: Call your travel agent or contact Mayflower Tours, 1225 Warren Ave., Downers Grove, IL 60515; 1-800-323-7604 or 708-960-3793.

SCI/NATIONAL RETIREES OF AMERICA

This agency, which began 32 years ago with trips to the Catskill resorts, now has a long list of group tours for seniors that range from one-day outings to 12-day cruises. The tours are all in the Northeast, depart midweek, and transport you by motorcoach. Choices of destination are myriad.

For information: SCI/National Retirees of America, 343 Merrick Ave., East Meadow, NY 11554; 1-800-427-7062 (in New York, 516-481-3939).

RETIRING IN MEXICO

Retire in Mexico (RIM), a travel company based in California, has organized a series of seminars and educational tours for people who are thinking about the possibility of retiring in Mexico, a neighboring country where the American dollar currently goes very far. Could Mexico provide a happy home for you? You can find out by signing on for a group visit to one or more of about a dozen south-of-the-border areas. You travel around the town and countryside by car or van with a small number of other potential retirees, and attend lectures on such subjects as health facilities, housing, investments, Mexican culture, and immigration.

On a typical tour, for example, you would spend three nights in Mexico City, then two each in San Miguel de Allende, Guanajuato, Morelia, and three in Guadalajara. There are other choices as well, all places with significant North American populations. In each area, you get conferences and tours conducted in English.

For information: Barvi Tours, 11658 Gateway Blvd., Los Angeles, CA 90064; 1-800-824-7102 (in California, 213-475-1861).

SENIOR ESCORTED TOURS

Specializing in vacations in Cape May, a beautiful little coastal town at the southern tip of New Jersey that abounds in Victoriana, this company also offers package trips to such places as Orlando, Florida, Boston, Nova

Scotia, Cape Cod, and the Catskills in New York—most of them including all meals. There are Caribbean and Alaskan cruises, as well as adventures in Australia, Hawaii, and the U.S. national parks.

For information: Call your travel agent or contact Senior Escorted Tours, PO Box 400, Cape May Court House, NJ 08210; 1-800-222-1254.

YUGOTOURS

It may not come as a surprise that Yugotours, owned by the Yugoslavian government, features trips to Yugoslavia when civil wars are not going on. It has become known for its "Prime of Your Life Vacations" for anybody who is retired or over 60 (plus companions of any age). The agency also offers tours to Spain and Portugal, London and Paris, Vienna, Prague and Budapest as well as Turkey and Malta.

Rates vary according to the time of year but are all-inclusive and very reasonable. These are "stay-put vacations," where you stay in one place for at least a week at a time. You may spend your entire vacation in one place or in a combination of places, and you may stay as many weeks as you like. You may customize your trip, taking it slow or becoming involved in the activities organized by the tour director in your hotel. Included in the package are breakfast and dinner.

For information: Call your travel agent or contact Yugotours, 350 Fifth Ave., New York, NY 10118; 1-800-223-5298 (in New York State, 212-563-2400).

CRUISING THE HIGH SEAS

Cruises have always appealed to the mature crowd. In fact, most sailings abound with people who are at least a few decades out of college. So, whatever trip you choose, you are sure to find suitable companionship. However, there are some special deals designed especially for you.

FANTASY CRUISES

If you are 65 or older, you may sign up for a Senior Saver cruise run by this cruise line and take a companion along for half price. In other words, a pair of passengers sharing a cabin will end up with a 25 percent reduction off the full fare. The offer applies, subject to availability, on the seven-night Caribbean cruises aboard the *Amerikanis* and the five-night trips to Mexico and the Caribbean on the *Britanis*.

For information: Call 1-800-423-2100.

CRUISE ESCORTS WANTED

Because single men of a certain age are mighty scarce among the traveling population, especially on board ship, a few cruise lines offer free travel or almost-free travel to carefully chosen unattached men over 50 who meet rigorous criteria. These unpaid hosts—usually retired professionals—encourage mingling among the passengers; serve as dancing, dining or bridge partners; act as escorts for shore trips; and generally socialize—without favoritism or romantic entanglements, we are assured—with the single women on board.

There are always many more applicants than spots for them, so don't be surprised if you are not encouraged to apply.

Royal Cruise Line has a roster of screened 50-plus men to act as unofficial hosts on its cruise ships. With a usual ratio of one host to 10 single women aboard, these congenial fellows do their best to see that the lone women travelers socialize with the other passengers and have a good time.

For information: Host Program, Royal Cruise Line, 1 Maritime Plaza, Ste. 1400, San Francisco, CA 94111.

The Delta Queen Steamboat Co., which makes about 50 cruises a year up and down the Mississippi River, taking you back in time aboard huge paddle-wheelers, recruits mature and responsible hosts, assigning two to each trip to help single women enjoy their voyage.
For information: Karp Enterprises Inc., 2139 University Drive, Coral Springs, FL 33071.

Sun Lines takes along several "dance hosts" on all of its longer, more expensive winter cruises. Their assignment is to dance with all the women who'd like to get out on the dance floor but haven't brought partners along.
For information: Host Program, Sun Line Cruises, 1 Rockefeller Plaza, New York, NY 10020.

Royal Viking Line's cruise ships recruit a number of gentlemen hosts to socialize, without romantic involvement, with the single women on board. They are there to participate in all the activities, from dancing and games to excursions ashore.
For information: Cruise Entertainment Dept., Kloster Cruise Ltd, 95 Merrick Way, Coral Gables, FL 33134.

Regency Cruises now takes a few male hosts along on its longer cruises, asking them to circulate among the guests and see that everyone has a good trip. Mostly retired professionals who have been selectively chosen, the hosts act as hospitality directors.
For information: Entertainment Manager, Regency Cruises, 8880 NW 20th St., Miami, FL 33172.

Merry Widow Dance Cruises, out of Tampa, runs several cruises a year for single women who were born to dance. Aboard ship are gentlemen hosts, one for every five women, whose job it is to whirl the passengers around the dance floor.
For information: Merry Widows Dance Cruises, 1515 N. Westshore Blvd., Tampa, FL 33607; 813-289-5923.

DANCE CRUISES

Designed for women from 50 to 90 who love to dance but don't have partners, the Merry Widows Dance Cruises runs several cruises every year to such places as the Caribbean, the Orient, Alaska, Greece and the Mediterranean, and the South Pacific. The trips range from seven days to 18. Under the auspices of the AAA Auto Club South, the cruises take along one male professional dancer for every five women on the trip. Each woman receives a dance card that rotates her partners every night throughout the cruise, whether she's a beginner or a polished dancer. The men are also rotated at the dinner tables so everyone gets the pleasure of their (platonic) company. You don't have to be a widow and you don't even have to know the cha-cha to have fun on these trips.

For information: Call your travel agent or contact Merry Widows Dance Cruises, 515 N. Westshore Blvd., Tampa, FL 33607; 813-289-5923.

PREMIER CRUISE LINES

You'll get a 10 percent discount on all of this line's cruises to Nassau and the Abacos if you are 60 and so will a traveling companion who shares your cabin. This also applies to The Big Red Boat that combines a three-day cruise with three days at Disney World in Orlando. You get free admission to the Magic Kingdom, Epcot Center, and Spaceport USA plus a rental car with unlimited mileage.

For information: Call your travel agent or contact Premier Cruise Lines, PO Box 573, Cape Canaveral, FL 32920; 1-800-327-7113.

SEA ESCAPE CRUISE LINES

If you're spending time in Florida and you have passed your 55th birthday, you may want to take advantage of the discounts on the one-day cruises run by this line. These short cruises leave from Miami or Fort Lauderdale and take you to Freeport or Bimini. All meals for the day are included.

For information: Call 1-800-327-7400 (in Florida, 1-800-432-0900).

SINGLEWORLD

Singleworld caters to unattached people who like to cruise the seas and spend time ashore sight-seeing, shopping, and sunning. Its trips are segregated according to age groups: 20 to 33, 29 to 49, and "all ages" (the last means you). Using major cruise lines and charging fares that are usually well below the regular tariffs, Singleworld schedules its trips at nonpeak times—usually in fall and early winter. At this moment, destinations include Caribbean ports as well as Cancún and Cozumel in Mexico, and cruises to the Far East.

Cruise passengers are guaranteed lower berths, the first sitting in the dining room, exclusive shore excursions, and special activities such as cocktail parties just for your crowd. A special escort is sent along on every cruise to organize shipboard activities and shore excursions and, in general, to make sure all goes well. Accommodations for solo travelers are arranged on a shared basis, meaning that you'll be assigned a suitable roommate if you haven't brought your own, and you pay no single supplement.

To participate, you must pay an annual membership fee of $25.

For information: Call your travel agent or contact Singleworld, PO Box 1999, Rye, NY 10580; 1-800-223-6490 or 914-967-3334.

SOUTH FLORIDA CRUISES

This cruise distributor specializes in bargain trips to the Caribbean, Mexico, South America, the Panama Canal, Europe, Alaska, the South Pacific, and the Far East, giving passengers substantially reduced rates. Its method is to purchase large blocks of space on brandname cruise lines and pass some of the savings along. What's more, it has declared it will give you an *additional* discount of about $50 per cabin if you are over 50 years of age and mention the "Unbelievably Good Deals and Great Adventures Special." In other words, say you found this information in this book!

For information: South Florida Cruises, Inc., 3561 NW 53rd Court, Fort Lauderdale, FL 33309; 1-800-327-SHIP (in Florida, 305-739-SHIP).

SIGHT-SEEING BY RAIL

Traveling by rail is a comfortable way to see the country, more leisurely than flying and more spacious than going by bus. But we know of only one tour operator offering a special deal to mature travelers.

OMNI SENIOR RAIL TOURS

You can tour the United States by rail at group rates with Omni Senior Rail Tours, an agency that runs many trips originating in Chicago for people over 50. You'll go by Amtrak. For local sight-seeing excursions, you'll travel by motorcoach. The tours of about 35 people are escorted and include transportation, hotels, many meals, sight-seeing trips, and entertainment. If you start from a city other than Chicago, you will be met in the Windy City, or you may join the tours along the way.

The itineraries include travel to Las Vegas, California, Santa Fe, Arizona's national parks, and a tour of eastern Canada.

For information: Call your travel agent or contact OmniTours, 104 Wilmot Rd., Deerfield, IL 60015; 1-800-962-0060 or 708-374-0088.

SPECIAL TRIPS TO ISRAEL

Israel is a favorite travel destination for many over-50 travelers, so several tour operators and Jewish organizations have designed visits especially for them. The trips are usually at least a couple of weeks long and organized in a leisurely fashion with plenty of free time.

AMERICAN JEWISH CONGRESS

The AJC runs lots of trips everywhere from the Caribbean to Australia but specializes in Israel. Its longer trips, especially the 15-day "Israel Slow and Easy" tour, are designed especially for people with plenty of time for an easygoing itinerary and so tend to appeal to older travelers. Traveling alone? You may want to choose AJC's special singles trips. There are several departures a year for singles between the ages of 39 and 55 and others for single adventurers over the age of 55.

For information: American Jewish Congress, 15 E. 84th St., New York, NY 10028; 1-800-221-4694 (in New York State, 212-879-4588, 516-752-1186, or 914-328-0018).

EL AL

The Israeli airline not only flies (at 60, you'll get a senior-citizen discounted fare) but also packages trips. Its 22-day "Israel at Leisure Tours" for people over 50 spend time in Tel Aviv, Jerusalem, and the Galilee, all with English-speaking guides.

The Jewish Heritage Tour to eastern Europe (Prague and Budapest) and Israel is designed to give American Jews an opportunity to explore their roots and is planned with older travelers in mind.

For information: Call your travel agent or contact El Al, 850 Third Ave., New York, NY 10022; 1-800-352-5786 (in New York, 212-768-9200).

Chapter Six
Singles on the Road

Lots of over-50s love to travel but don't have anybody to do it with. If you're single, single once again, or have a spouse who isn't the traveling kind, there's no need to give up your dreams of faraway places simply because you don't want to travel alone. There are many organizations and packagers ready to come to your aid. Some offer special trips for mature singles where you mingle with others on their own, and many help match you up with a fellow traveler who is also looking for a compatible person with whom to share adventures, a room, and expenses. Traveling with another person is usually more fun and certainly less expensive than going alone because you share double accommodations, thereby avoiding the single supplement, which can be substantial.

MATCHMAKERS

TRAVEL COMPANION EXCHANGE
Specializing in finding the right travel companion from all age groups from 18 to 85, TCE matches up single, divorced, or widowed travelers for joint adventures. Operated by travel expert Jens Jurgen, who is always thinking up new ways of matchmaking and making traveling more fun, this organization, the largest and

most enduring of its kind, works hard at making compatible connections and has been very successful.

Members receive chatty bimonthly newsletters stuffed with travel tips and frequent listings of people actively seeking travel partners. For more details on those who seem good possibilities, you send for Profile Pages—or others send for yours—so that you may judge suitability for yourself. You do your own matchmaking. Mr. Jurgen suggests you talk by telephone, correspond, meet, and, even better, take a short trip together before setting out on a major adventure. By the way, TCE gives free memberships to unmarried older men! And, if you wish, you may subscribe to the newsletter only.

For information: Travel Companion Exchange Inc., PO Box 833, Amityville, NY 11701; 516-454-0880.

GOLDEN COMPANIONS

Exclusively for travelers over 49, Golden Companions will help you find company to wander with, perhaps another solo voyager or a small group that moves out together. "It is for those who do not want to travel alone, for those who do not want to travel in large groups, and for those wishing to expand their existing circle of travel friends," says Joanne Buteau, its founder. Membership entitles you to a bimonthly newsletter, the networking service, a mailing list, and a mail-exchange service. This club gets you discounts on some tours for mature travelers and organizes its own cruises and tours for its members.

For information: Golden Companions, PO Box 754, Pullman, WA 99163; 509-334-9351.

MATURE TRAVEL MATES
The newest matchmaker on the scene is Mature Travel Mates, a Florida network that helps people who are 49 or older hook up with other mature singles looking for traveling companions. As a member, you'll get profiles of possible candidates with whom you may then correspond to see if you are compatible. You will also get discounts on cruises and will receive frequent newsletters that include information about the club and its services. MTM arranges group cruises for its members or you may make your own travel arrangements.
For information: Mature Travel Mates, PO Box 26832, Tamarac, FL 33320; 407-338-4203.

PARTNERS-IN-TRAVEL
This group is devoted to making travel a happier experience for solo travelers through contacts and connections. With a newsletter and its Match Up service, the goal is to link up travel companions, most of them in the "mature" category. The newsletter prints mini-listings that will be followed up, upon request, by more detailed profiles of members seeking travel companions. An additional service is a Vacation Home Exchange program available to members who wish to extend hospitality and/or accommodations to fellow members.
For information: Partners-in-Travel, PO Box 491145, Los Angeles, CA 90049; 213-476-4869.

TOURS FOR SOLO TRAVELERS

Several tour operators and agencies specializing in escorted trips for people in their prime will try to find you a roommate (of the same sex) to share your room or cabin so you will not have to pay a supplement. And, if they can't manage to find a suitable roommate, they will usually reduce the supplement even though you'll have your own private room. Some run singles trips as well. In any case, keep in mind that you'll hardly have time or opportunity to be lonely on the typical escorted tour run by these agencies. If you are planning an extended stay in one place, however, you may have more need for company.

For more about the tour operators listed below, see Chapter 5. Other companies may offer the same singles-matching service, though they don't make a point of it, so always ask about it if you're interested.

AMERICAN JEWISH CONGRESS

Singles who would like to travel to Israel or other places such as Spain, England, or Eastern Europe with a group of solo travelers in their own age range should check out the trips run by the American Jewish Congress. There are trips every year for singles aged 35 to 55 and several for singles over 55. The age requirements are not ironbound—you choose the group with which you feel most comfortable. If you ask AJC to find you a roommate, and it can't, it guarantees a single room without the single supplement.

For information: American Jewish Congress, 15 E. 84th St., New York, NY 10028; 1-800-221-4694 (in New York state, 212-879-4588; 516-752-1186; 914-328-0018).

CLASSIC SINGLES NETWORK

If you want to avoid the possibility of being a single person on a tour filled with couples and would prefer traveling with other "mature singles," check this agency out. Part of Olson Travel, it offers escorted packaged tours for small groups of older solo travelers to many parts of the world that currently include Italy, France, the Orient, Hawaii, and Egypt. Hotels are first class or deluxe, you share a twin room, and breakfast and some other meals are included. Several tours are offered for holiday seasons—around Thanksgiving and Christmas—when many older singles like to be on the move.

For information: Call your travel agent or 1-800-421-2255 (in California, 1-800-421-5785).

GOLDEN AGE TRAVELLERS

An over-50 club, Golden Age Travellers will enroll you in its "Roommates Wanted" list if you wish help in finding a companion with whom to share the costs and the fun.

For information: Golden Age Travellers, Pier 27, The Embarcadero, San Francisco, CA 94111; 1-800-258-8880 (in California, 1-800-652-1683).

GRAND CIRCLE TRAVEL

Grand Circle, which concentrates on over-50 travel packages, tries to match singles with appropriate roommates if they request them. If there are none at hand, you will be charged only half the single supplement for your own room. And on several of its Live Abroad Vacations departure dates, you will not pay the single supplement at all.

This company also offers a Pen Pal section in its catalogs that allows clients to make new friends and perhaps find people to travel with.

For information: Grand Circle Travel, 347 Congress St., Boston, MA 02210; 1-800-248-3737.

MAYFLOWER TOURS

Another travel operator with mature travelers as its focus, Mayflower will also get you a roommate if you like or, if that's not possible, absorbs the cost of the single-room supplement. You then pay the regular twin rate.

For information: Mayflower Tours, 1225 Warren Ave., Downers Grove, IL 60515; 1-800-323-7604 or 708-960-3430.

SAGA HOLIDAYS

A tour company specializing in trips for people over 60 (see Chapter 5), Saga Holidays will try to find a roommate for you on its escorted tours and cruises so you won't have to pay the single supplement. It also schedules several exclusive Singles Departures each season. On these, the single supplement prices are reduced.

For information: Saga Holidays, 120 Boylston St., Boston, MA 02116; 1-800-343-0273.

SINGLEWORLD

To help you enjoy vacationing in the company of others, while avoiding single-supplement fees, Singleworld offers its members cruises and tours specifically for solo travelers. Members, who pay a membership fee of $25 a year, also receive a quarterly newsletter. You will fit best into Singleworld's trips for "all ages," a category that attracts the over-50s.

For information: Singleworld, P.O. Box 1999, Rye, NY 10580; 1-800-223-6490 or 914-967-3334.

SOLO FLIGHTS

This travel agency arranges vacations specifically for single travelers of all ages, with much of its clientele on the far side of 50. It keeps track of the best tours, cruises, packages, groups, and rates for single people, and so with one telephone call or a letter you can find out—at no charge—what's out there that interests you, from weekend getaways to full-length vacations offered by major tour operators, including Club Med, as well as lesser-known possibilities. Of course, the agency will do your booking.

For information: Solo Flights, 127 S. Compo Rd., Westport, CT 06880; 203-226-9993.

SUDDENLY SINGLE TOURS

This agency offers first-class-all-the-way group tours in this country and abroad exclusively for people "over 40" who have suddenly become single again in midlife. Its travel programs "are designed with your maturity, tastes, and needs in mind." Departures are from the Midwest and New York. The guided trips, both in this country and in foreign lands, are designed to provide deluxe accommodations and private rooms for everyone.

For information: Suddenly Single Tours, Ltd., 161 Dreiser Loop, New York, NY 10475; 212-379-8800.

HOOK-UPS FOR LONE RVers

RVers who travel alone in their motor homes or vans can hook up with others in the same circumstances when they join one of the groups mentioned below. Both provide opportunities to travel together or to meet at campgrounds on the road, making friends with fellow travelers, and having fun.

LONERS OF AMERICA

LOA stresses that it is not a matchmaking organization but rather a club for single RVers who want to travel together. In existence only a few years, it now has 29 chapters throughout the country and 1,400 members from their 40s to their 90s, almost all retired and all widowed, divorced, or otherwise single. Many of them live year-round in their motor homes or vans, and others hit the road only occasionally. They camp together, rally together, caravan together, often meeting at special campgrounds that cater to solo RVers.

A not-for-profit member-operated organization, the club sends you an annual membership directory and a lively bimonthly newsletter that lets you know about campouts and rallies all over the country. The chapters organize their own events as well. Currently, dues are $20 a year plus a $5 registration fee for new members. **For information:** Loners of America, Rte. 2, Box 85E, Ellsinore, MO 63937; 314-322-5548.

LONERS ON WHEELS

Most of the members of Loners on Wheels, a 54-chapter national recreational club, are retired and over 50, but the only ironclad rule for membership is that you are single! "There are literally hundreds of campouts each year sponsored by the chapters, as well as about 12 large rallies each year in various parts of the country and Canada," according to its literature. All kinds of RVs are included, as well as all kinds of people who participate in all kinds of recreational and educational activities. Aside from the outings, there are Loners on Wheels campgrounds in the Ozarks, Florida, and California.
For information: Write to Loners on Wheels, PO Box 1355, Poplar Bluff, MO 63901; 314-785-2420.

Chapter Seven
Airfares: Improving with Age

One thing that improves with age—yours—is airfare. Almost every airline in existence now offers discounted senior fares and sometimes they are the best deals around. The airlines are currently using four ways of attracting mellow travelers: clubs with discounts, discounts without clubs, unlimited-mileage passes, and coupon books (travel bargains that are hard to beat, particularly if you are planning long trips). That's because we have proved to be the hottest travel market to tap today. We are a vast and growing group of careful consumers with money in our pockets and time on our hands during slack off-peak periods, just when the airlines like to fill up seats.

The minimum age for senior fares is 50, but most of the discounts are offered later—when you are 60 or 62 or 65. Most programs allow a companion of any age, regardless of sex or relationship, to travel with you at the same reduced fare, although occasionally that person must pay a fee for the privilege. In some cases, however, your younger companion must be married to you to get the slashed prices.

Several airlines have arrangements with car-rental companies and hotel chains to provide discounts on these, too. (See Chapter 8 for more on car rentals and Chapter 10 for more on hotels and motels.)

But, first, keep in mind:

▶ Always ask your travel agent or the airline reservations clerk to get you the *lowest possible fare*. Mention the fact that you qualify for a senior discount, but be prepared to jump ship if you can get a better deal by going with a special promotional rate or a super super-saver fare—although sometimes your discount can cut these lowest fares even lower. Many airlines now offer special promotional fares for seniors during off-peak seasons. Watch for these sales; they are usually the cheapest way to go, especially when you can deduct the airline's regular senior discount from them.

▶ Keep in mind that the restrictions you must fly by may not be worth the savings. Always examine the fees and conditions and decide whether you can live with them. There may be blackout periods around major holidays when you can't use your discount, departures only on certain days or hours, restrictions on the season of the year, or stiff penalties for flight changes. In some plans, you must travel the entire distance on one airline even if connections are poor. It's not easy to sort out the offers because some carriers give better discounts but more hassles—or vice versa—so make comparisons before arriving at a decision.

▶ Before you decide to buy a yearly pass or a coupon book, figure out how many trips you're likely to make during the next year. Unless you see clear savings, you are better off with individual tickets. But if you travel frequently, or would do so once you had the pass, then it could be an excellent buy.

▶ Book your flights as early as possible for the best fares and the most available seats (frequently, the number of seats is severely limited). Try to couple your senior discounts with ultimate supersaver fares, which require 30-day advance purchase and include other restrictions on length of stay, and days on which you may fly.

▶ Be prepared to present a membership card (if you are flying as a member of a club) and a valid proof of age at the check-in counter. It's possible that your discount will not be honored if you don't have that proof with you, and you will have to pay the difference.

Now for some of the potential bargain offers. Be advised that airfares and airline policies often change overnight, so always call the airline that interests you for an update.

U.S. SKIES: MAJOR AIRLINES

AMERICAN AIRLINES

American Airlines offers another good deal if you are 62 and travel enough in a year's time to make it worthwhile. That's its Senior TrAAveler Coupon Books, which give you four-coupon or eight-coupon books at low per-trip prices. Traded in for a ticket, each coupon is good for travel one way in the 48 contiguous states as well as Puerto Rico, St. Thomas, and St. Croix. Hawaii requires two coupons each way.

You may travel any day of the week, but you must buy your tickets at least 14 days in advance of your flight. There is no refund on the coupons and no change of itinerary on one-way tickets, although if you don't take your reserved flight, you may use the ticket for a standby seat. On round trips, you may change your outbound flight at least 14 days before the flight for a $25 service charge. You may change your return any time for a $25 service charge. Seats are limited, but you will be entitled to frequent-flyer credits for all the miles you fly.

American Eagle, a commuter airline, is part of American Airlines, and these privileges apply to its flights as well.

For information: Call your travel agent or 1-800-433-7300 for reservations or Senior Discounts. For the Senior TrAAveler Coupon Books, call 1-800-237-7981.

CONTINENTAL AIRLINES

You, and a travel mate of any age, will get a flat 10 percent discount on Continental Airlines on all fares, even the lowest, if you are 62. Just ask for it and be ready to prove your age. You'll be eligible for frequent-flyer credits with these tickets.

Or, if you do a lot of traveling, consider the Freedom Passport, which is available in two varieties. The domestic passport gives you virtually unlimited travel for a year in the United States, Canada, and the Caribbean, either coach or first class, at good savings if you make many flights within those twelve months. In addition, there are low-cost options that allow you to add on trips to Mexico, Central America, Hawaii, Europe, or the South Pacific. The global version of the passport, which of course costs more, lets you fly all over the world, including the United States. You may buy the passport at age 62.

Some restrictions to using the Freedom Passport: You may fly to the same city only three times during the year. Seats are limited, and there are some blackout periods around major holidays. You are entitled to one one-way trip per week and must stay over a Saturday night. For domestic flights, travel is restricted to noon

Monday through noon Thursday and all day Saturday, and reservations may be made no earlier than seven days in advance. For international flights, hours are all day Monday through Thursday and Saturday, and reservations can be made no earlier than 30 days in advance. No frequent-flyer credits are given for tickets purchased with the passport. However, a Companion Passport is also available for the same price for your travel mate, who may be younger but must always be the same person.

A third option offered by Continental is its Freedom Trips for people over 62. These are booklets of four or eight low-cost coupons that may be traded in for tickets on flights anywhere the airline goes within the United States, Mexico, the Caribbean, and Bermuda. Flights to Hawaii, Alaska, Mexico, the Caribbean, and Bermuda will cost you two coupons each way. You must make reservations at least 14 days in advance, but you may fly any day of the week except for blackout periods around major holidays. You will receive frequent-flyer credits on these flights.

For information: Call your travel agent or 1-800-525-0280 for reservations or 1-800-441-1135 for the Freedom Passport.

DELTA AIRLINES
The good deal offered by Delta Airlines is its Young at Heart Coupon Program for travelers over 62, which gives you a book of coupons good for one-way travel at low prices if you use them all within a year. The costs are low for four coupons and even lower per trip for eight coupons. One coupon will take you anywhere the airline flies in the continental United States and Puerto Rico; two coupons are required to fly to Alaska or Ha-

waii. You may fly any day of the week, but seats are limited, so book ahead. Reservations must be made at least 14 days in advance of your flight; with less notice, however, you may travel standby. You'll get frequent-flyer credits for the miles you fly.

For information: Call your travel agent or 1-800-221-1212.

DELTA SHUTTLE

For shuttle flights to or from New York and Washington or Boston, you may buy the Senior Pass, currently priced at about half of the regular fare for other passengers—that is, if you are 65 and can provide evidence of that fact a half hour before flight time. And yes, you will get frequent-flyer credits. With the pass, you may fly from 10:00 A.M. to 2:30 P.M. Monday through Friday and all day Saturday and Sunday.

For information: Call your travel agent or 1-800-221-1212.

NORTHWEST AIRLINES

For passengers over 62, Northwest offers its Ultrafare Coupon Books, with each coupon good for a one-way flight in the continental United States and Canada. Flights to Hawaii, Alaska, or the Caribbean cost two coupons per one-way trip. If you use all your coupons within a year, the per-trip cost is a real bargain, especially if you fly cross-country. You may fly any time, any day, but you must make your reservations at least 14 days in advance. Seats are limited, however, so book your flights as early as you can. You are entitled to frequent-flyer credits.

For information: Call your travel agent or 1-800-225-2525.

TWA (TRANSWORLD AIRLINES)

This airline reduces the fare by 10 percent for travelers over 62 and a companion of any age on almost all flights in the U.S. and Puerto Rico and some to Europe as well (England and Italy, for example). Ask for the discount when you make your reservations. You'll get frequent-flyer credits for your mileage.

The Senior Travel Pak is another alternative offered by TWA. This gives you four one-way domestic coupons at a remarkably low price. A younger traveling companion gets them for the same price. Each coupon may be exchanged for a one-way ticket on flights in the United States and to Puerto Rico. In addition, you get a bonus coupon that allows you to purchase a round-trip ticket to Europe at a good discount. Within the lower 48 states, you may fly any time except all day Thursday or 12 noon to 7:00 P.M. on Friday and Sunday. To Hawaii and San Juan, flying days are limited to Tuesday, Wednesday, or Thursday only. Travel to Hawaii costs two coupons each way from any mainland point, as does any flight that's more than 2,000 miles and is made from August 1 through August 30.

TWA is the first airline to come out with companion coupon books to go along with its senior coupons. If a traveler who is over 62 buys a book of four coupons, a younger person can buy four companion coupons to be used only when they travel together. The companion books cost more than the senior books, but they are still a bargain. All four companion coupons must be used by the same person.

For information: Call your travel agent or 1-800-221-2000 for reservations.

UNITED AIRLINES

United Airlines' senior travel club, called Silver Wings Plus, is open to you if you are over 60 and includes many benefits. You may become a lifetime member for $150, but you get your money back in the form of three $50 discount certificates for travel within a year and 3,000 frequent-flyer miles. Or for $75, you may join for three years and receive three $25 certificates plus 1,000 frequent-flyer miles. With your membership you'll receive discounts on hotels, rental cars, cruises, and travel packages, plus offers of special discounted programs. You will be automatically enrolled in the mileage-plus program, get credits for miles, and receive the *Silver Wings Plus* newsletter.

On your 62nd birthday, the Silver Wings Plus program starts giving you a 10 percent discount on all applicable published fares to destinations in the United States, Canada, Mexico, Singapore, Australia, New Zealand, Taiwan, China, Korea, Thailand, the Philippines, and even a few major cities in Europe. Your membership also allows you a discount of 10 percent on United Express, British Midlands Airlines, Alitalia, Australian Airlines, Mt. Cook Airlines of New Zealand, KLM, and Iberia flights to Europe.

Another good deal for travelers over the age of 62 is United's Silver TravelPac program. You may choose books of four or eight coupons at low per-trip fares. Each coupon is good for a one-way trip on United or United Express within the 48 contiguous states and to and from San Juan. Two coupons are required each way to Hawaii and most flights to Alaska. You may travel any day of the week.

Seats are limited and you must make your reservations at least 14 days in advance or travel on standby. Your coupons may be exchanged for tickets up to the day of your departure. Yes, you will earn frequent-flyer points for your mileage when you use the coupons. One more point: Mileage Plus Premier members may combine their coupons with 500- and 1,000-mile upgrade certificates.

For information: Call your travel agent or 1-800-241-6522 for reservations. Call 1-800-628-2868 for United Silver Wings Plus; or 1-800-633-6563 for United Silver TravelPac.

USAir

A good choice is USAir's Senior Discount Coupon Books. At a low per-trip cost, you may buy a book of four one-way coupons, or at even less per trip, a book of eight one-way coupons. Each coupon may be traded for a ticket to any destination within the continental United States or Puerto Rico, including flights on affiliated commuter lines. The coupon books may be purchased when you are 62. You must use them up within a year of purchase and book your trips at least 14 days before you travel. If you don't have the 14 days, you may use your coupon for a standby ticket. There are some blackout periods around holidays, but you'll accumulate mileage points in the frequent-flyer program.

Bonus: your coupons may also be traded for tickets for grandchildren ages two through eleven who travel with you.

For information: Call your travel agent or 1-800-428-4322.

USAir SHUTTLE
If you are over 65, you may fly at half price on this airline's shuttle flights between New York and Boston or Washington, D.C., if you are willing to travel off-peak. You may fly Monday through Friday from 10:00 A.M. to 2:00 P.M. and 7:00 P.M. to midnight, as well as all day Saturday or Sunday.

Even more cost effective for mature travelers who fly the shuttle frequently is the Senior FlightPass, which is good for a year's use. This is a book of five or ten coupons, each of which may be traded for a ticket on a flight that is taking off during the off-peak hours (Monday through Friday from 10:00 A.M. to 2:00 P.M. and 7:00 P.M. to midnight, as well as all day Saturday or Sunday).

For information: Call your travel agent or 1-800-428-4322.

U.S. REGIONAL AIRLINES

ALASKA AIRLINES
Alaska Airlines gives you, at 62, and a traveling companion a 10 percent discount on most flights in and out of the state. Sometimes, during the off-seasons, the special senior fares are even better. Inquire about them before making a decision.

This airline also sells a Senior Coupon Book that allows travelers 62 and over to buy sets of four or eight coupons at good prices. Trade the coupons in for tickets on flights to any of its destinations except Mexico and the Soviet Union at least 14 days before you travel. You will be entitled to frequent-flyer points when you use the coupons.

For information: Call your travel agent or 1-800-426-0333.

ALOHA AIRLINES

Aloha, which flies only among the Hawaiian Islands, charges those over 60 a fare that is a few dollars cheaper than the full fare for everyone else.

For information: Call your travel agent or 1-800-367-5250.

AMERICA WEST

This airline has two offers for you at 62. The first is its Senior Saver Pack, a coupon book good for a year that currently gives you four one-way flights at discounted prices wherever it flies within the continental U.S., or eight one-way trips for even less per trip. Two coupons are required for flights to Hawaii. Travel days are limited to noon on Monday through noon on Thursday and all day Saturday. Seats are limited, and reservations must be made 14 days in advance. There are some blackout periods.

In addition, America West offers its Senior Fare that gives you a discount of 10 percent on normal coach fares. Ask whether it is the lowest fare available to you on the days you want to fly.

For information: Call your travel agent or 1-800-247-5692.

HAWAIIAN AIR

Here, too, you may fly inter-island for less than the regular fare if you are 60. You are also entitled to a 10 percent discount off any published fare on flights to and from the mainland U.S., and so is your traveling companion.

For information: Call your travel agent or 1-800-367-5320.

MIDWEST EXPRESS
Ten percent is taken off the fare for people over 65 on all
fares to all destinations. The discount also applies to
Skyway Airlines.
For information: Call your travel agent or 1-800-452-
2022.

SOUTHWEST AIRLINES
Flying mainly in the southwestern United States, this
company offers special low fares to travelers over 65 on
all flights. If you make 20 one-way trips with Southwest,
by the way, you'll get a free round-trip anywhere it flies.
For information: Call your travel agent or 1-800-531-
5601

GOOD DEALS ON CANADIAN AIRLINES

AIR CANADA
If you are over 60, you and a traveling companion of any
age are eligible for a 10 percent reduction on the lowest
applicable fare, including special sales. You will also get
frequent-flyer points for your mileage.

Air Canada's Freedom Flyer program is another good
choice for travelers over the age of 60. It provides you
with two choices. The first is the Multi-Stop option package, which gives you reduced fares on Air Canada and
its connector airlines for extensive visits to four or more
cities in North America during one trip.

The second option is the Single-Trip package, at reduced prices, that gives you coupon books good for four
or eight one-way tickets to be used on several separate
trips. Reservations for both kinds of packages must be

made at least two weeks before departure. You will get frequent-flyer mileage on these flights.

All of these Air Canada discounts are available to traveling companions, any age, when they travel with you. You are also entitled to a range of services including discounts for Avis car rentals, accommodations at Hilton International and Holiday Inn hotels, and seven-day unlimited travel passes on Greyhound's Canadian route network.
For information: Call your travel agent or 1-800-776-3000.

CANADIAN AIRLINES INTERNATIONAL
Your discount here, if you are 62 or older, is 10 percent off any fare on round-trip tickets to destinations within Canada and the United States (except Hawaii) or between Canada and the United Kingdom. A traveling companion of any age can fly with you at the same fare. You get frequent-flyer credits for these flights, and there are no restrictions on time, day, or season. But, as with any discounted fares, remember to book early, as seats are limited.
For information: Call your travel agent or 1-800-426-7000.

GOOD DEALS ON FOREIGN AIRLINES

Again, always inquire about special senior discounts when you book a flight, even if you don't see them listed here. Airlines change their policies with very little notice. Your travel agent can provide current information.

AIR FRANCE

A 10 percent senior citizen discount is available to you at age 62 on Air France flights between the airline's nine major U.S. gateway cities and France. The discount is deducted from many fares, and all restrictions on these fares apply.

For information: Call your travel agent or 1-800-237-2747.

ALITALIA

If you are a member of United's Silver Wings Plus travel club and are over 65, you are eligible for a 10 percent discount on Alitalia flights.

For information: Call your travel agent or 1-800-223-5730.

BRITISH AIRWAYS

The Privileged Traveller Program offered by British Airways is a really good deal for those of us who are over 60 and our traveling mates who are over 50. For a yearly fee of $25, you receive a card entitling you to 10 percent savings on point-to-point airfares between the U.S. and most cities in Europe, whether you fly economy, club, first class, or Concorde. Just make your reservations using your membership number. The discount even applies to promotional sale fares to destinations in the United Kingdom.

You will also be eligible for 10 percent (or more) off British Airways Holidays land tours; Forte Hotels in the U.S. and the U.K.; cruises on the *QE2* and other Cunard ships; travel on the Venice-Simplon Orient Express; and Avis car rentals. An added feature: as a Privileged Traveller you may preboard the plane. The membership card also serves as your proof of age and contains a record of your meal and seat preferences as well as any special medical needs.

And here's another big plus: There are no penalties for canceling or changing your flight plans if you do so at the start of your travel. Nor are there blackout periods. You will receive frequent-flyer credits for the flights as well.

For information: Call your travel agent or the Privileged Traveller program at 1-800-828-7797. For British Airways reservations, call 1-800-247-9297.

EL AL

Anyone over the age of 60 is entitled to El Al's Golden Age Fare, which gives you a discount of about 15 percent off the regular Apex fare to Israel. You may stay for up to two months and may make one stopover in Europe. A 14-day advance purchase is required, and there is a $50 fee for changing your return flight.

But, before accepting this deal, check out whether the cheaper Superapex fare (with a maximum stay of 21 days) will work out better for you.

For information: Call your travel agent or 1-800-223-6700 or 212-768-9200.

IBERIA

If you are a member of United's Silver Wings Plus travel club, you will get 10 percent off most published fares on Iberia.

For information: Call your travel agent or 1-800-772-4642.

KLM ROYAL DUTCH AIRLINES

KLM lowers the fares somewhat for travelers over 60 and their spouses on flights from the United States to several cities in the Netherlands—but only in the off-season. KLM also participates in the United's Silver Wings Plus travel club, entitling members to a 10 percent discount on all applicable published fares.

For information: Call your travel agent or 1-800-777-5553.

LUFTHANSA

At age 62, you can get a 10 percent reduction on most coach or Apex fares for yourself and a younger travel mate, on flights from gateway cities in the U.S. to Germany.

For information: Call your travel agent or 1-800-645-3880.

MEXICANA

A senior discount of 10 percent applies to all Mexicana fares between gateway cities in the U.S. and Mexico, including stopovers, except in July and August. You must be 62, but your traveling companion may be younger and get the same rate. There are blackouts around major holidays.

For information: Call your travel agent or 1-800-531-7921.

SABENA (BELGIAN WORLD AIRLINES)

Special senior fares are the offer from Sabena on flights to Tel Aviv. You must be 60 years old. At 62, you're also entitled to a 10 percent discount on some fares to European destinations. Another good deal is a 10 percent discount for members of United's Silver Wings Plus travel club.

For information: Call your travel agent or 1-800-950-1000.

SAS (SCANDINAVIAN AIRLINES)

There are no senior discounts on SAS from this continent to Scandinavia. However, if you are 65 you are entitled to a 50 percent discount on domestic flights within Sweden and a 25 percent discount on fares within Danish borders. In Norway, domestic flights are half price for you at the age of 67. Always take your passport along when you buy your tickets for proof of your age.

For information: Call your travel agent or 1-800-221-2350.

SWISSAIR

Swissair offers you a 10 percent discount on almost all fares on flights from its gateway cities in the U.S. to Switzerland. It's yours for the asking if you are over 62 and applies to a traveling companion as well.

For information: Call your travel agent or 1-800-221-4750.

TAP AIR PORTUGAL

The senior discount here, for those over 60, is minimal and is available only during the off-peak season, usually from September 15 until the end of May. You may fly any day of the week and get the same fare for a traveling companion.

For information: Call your travel agent or 1-800-221-7370.

Chapter Eight
Beating the Costs
of Car Rentals

N ever rent a car without getting a discount or a special promotional rate. Almost all car-rental agencies in the United States and Canada give them to all manner of customers, including those who belong to over-50 organizations (see Chapter 19) and airline senior clubs (see Chapter 7). The discount that's coming to you as a member can save you a lot of money. Refer to the membership material sent by the group to which you belong for specific information about your discount privileges.

But, first, keep in mind:

▶ Don't grab your member discount too hastily because you may belong to some other organization that will save you even more. Remember that you may be eligible for other discounts—frequent-flyer, auto club, or business discounts, for example—that are better than senior rates. And sometimes there are promotional "sales" that offer more. Ask your travel agent to find you the best deal. Or, on your own, always ask for the *lowest available rate* at that moment—mentioning, of course, the groups to which you belong.

▶ When you call to ask about rates or reservations, always be armed with your organization's ID number and your own membership card for reference.

▶ The savings may not be available at all locations, so you must check them out each time you make a reservation.

Here are the car-rental agencies that are currently offering you special rates or discounts.

ALAMO RENT A CAR
The Experienced Driver Discount—10 percent off the lowest available retail rate—is offered at all locations to members of AARP, Delta's Young at Heart program, United's Silver Wings Plus travel club, *and* anyone else who's over 50. Alamo offers other special discounts every year during the month of September; so if you're planning to travel at that time, check them out. A 24-hour advance reservation is required in all cases.
For information: Call 1-800-327-9633.

AVIS CAR RENTAL
Special rates, amounting to 5 to 10 percent off regular rates, are given to members of AARP and CARP (Canadian Association of Retired Persons).
For information: Call 1-800-331-1800.

BUDGET/SEARS RENT-A-CAR
Participating Budget/Sears locations give varying discounts to members of AARP and many other lesser-known 50-plus or senior groups.
For information: Call 1-800-527-0700.

DOLLAR RENT A CAR
Discounts, which vary according to location, are offered to AARP members at 50 and anyone else over 60.
For information: Call 1-800-800-4000.

HERTZ CAR RENTAL
If you are a member of AARP or Y.E.S., you will be entitled to savings, usually from 5 to 10 percent, on Hertz rental cars. In addition, Hertz gives discounts to members of United's Silver Wings Plus travel club, and Days Inns' September Days Club.
For information: Call 1-800-654-3131.

NATIONAL CAR RENTAL
With this rent-a-car agency, you can get special rates and discounts if you are a member of AARP.
For information: Call 1-800-328-4567.

THRIFTY CAR RENTAL
AARP members get a 10 percent discount on rentals any day of the week in the U.S. and 5 percent overseas. Members of CARP and Days Inns' September Days Club are also entitled to senior discounts.
For information: Call 1-800-367-2277.

Chapter Nine
Saving a Bundle on Trains, Buses, and Boats in North America

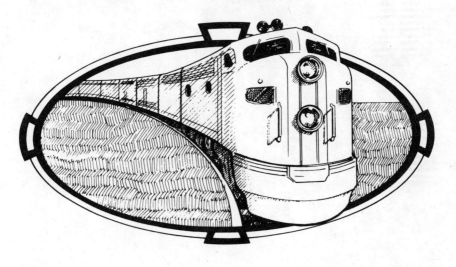

Getting around town, especially if you live in a city where driving is not a practical option, probably means depending on public transportation to get you from hither to yon. Remember that, once you reach a particular birthday—in most cases, your 60th or 65th—you can take advantage of some good senior markdowns on trains, buses, and subways (unfortunately, taxis have yet to join the movement). All you need is a Medicare card or a senior ID card issued by your city or county to play this game, which usually reduces fares by half. Although you may find it uncomfortable at the beginning to pull out that card and flash it at the bus driver or ticket agent, it soon becomes automatic and you will realize some nice savings.

Seniors can find bargains on long-distance rail and bus travel as well.

RIDING THE RAILS

Probably every commuter railroad in the United States and Canada gives older riders a break, although you may have to do your traveling during off-peak periods when the trains are not filled with go-getters rushing to and from their offices. Ask for your discount when you purchase your ticket.

As for serious long-distance travel, many mature travelers are addicted to the railroads, finding riding the rails a leisurely, relaxed, romantic, comfortable, economical, and satisfying way to make miles while enjoying the scenery.

So many passes and discounts on railroads are available to travelers heading for other parts of the world that sorting them out becomes confusing. But, once you do, they will help stretch your dollars while covering a lot of ground.

See the country-by-country section in Chapter 4 for the best deals on trains in foreign countries for travelers of a certain age. Also check out the sight-seeing trips run by Omni Senior Rail Tours (pages 58–59).

AMTRAK

To accommodate senior travelers, Amtrak offers a 15 percent discount on the lowest available coach fare to anyone 62 or older. Your trip must begin on a Monday, Tuesday, Wednesday, or Thursday, although necessary connections on the three peak travel days are allowed. The discount may not be used on Auto Train or Metroliner Service, but you may upgrade to first-class Club Service or sleeping accommodations using the senior coach fare as your base. The only blackout periods when the senior discount won't apply are on the day before Thanksgiving and from December 26 through December 31.

The lowest round-trip coach fares often sell out quickly, so always book train space well in advance. Not all fares are available on every train and some have restrictions.

Also, ask about new fare reductions for over-62s on Amtrak's air/rail travel plans.

For information: Call Amtrak at 1-800-USA-RAIL.

VIA RAIL CANADA

The government-owned Canadian passenger railroad offers you, at age 60, 10 percent off the regular coach fare every day of the year with no restrictions. Add this 10 percent to the 40 percent reduction on off-peak travel, available to all ages and applicable any day of the week except Friday and Sunday, and you end up with tickets that are half price. Tickets at the off-peak rate must be purchased at least five days in advance. However, the number of seats sold at this rate is limited, so plan ahead and buy your tickets as early as possible.

An additional program for the over-60 crowd is Via Rail Canada's Ambassador Club. It costs you nothing to join and offers you seasonal promotions as well as discounts on hotel accommodations that range from 25 to 50 percent. You'll also receive a quarterly newsletter. Pick up an application at a major railroad station, or write or call Via Rail for one

For information: Via Rail Canada, 2 Place Ville Marie, Montreal, Quebec, Canada H3B 2C9; 514-871-1331. For reservations, call the toll-free number for your region of the country (get the number for your area by dialing 1-800-555-1212). .

LET THEM DO THE DRIVING: GO BY BUS

Never, never board a bus without showing the driver your senior ID card, because even the smallest bus lines in the tiniest communities in this country and abroad give senior discounts, usually half fare. In Europe, your senior rail pass is often valid on major motorcoach lines as well, so always be sure to ask.

GREYHOUND-TRAILWAYS BUS LINES

If you decide to let Greyhound do the driving, you are entitled to a 10 percent reduction on regular fares Monday through Thursday and 5 percent Friday to Sunday once you have passed your 65th birthday. But always keep in mind that Greyhound-Trailways offers occasional "specials," promotional fares that are even lower than you'll get with your senior discount, so be sure to ask for the *lowest available fare* at the time you want to travel. Your senior discount, by the way, may not be applied to promotional fares.

For information: Call your local Greyhound-Trailways reservations office.

GRAY LINE TOURS

Gray Line is an association of many small independent motorcoach lines throughout the country, all of which offer sight-seeing and package tours. Most, but not all, of them give a 15 percent discount on half- and full-day sight-seeing tours to members of AARP at age 50 and sometimes other seniors as well. Find out if you qualify before buying your ticket.

For information: Call the Gray Line Tours office in your area.

VOYAGEUR COLONIAL LTD.

This Canadian motorcoach line's Club 60 offers you a third off the regular one-way bus fares throughout the provinces of Quebec and Ontario, without prior reservations, on Monday through Thursday and Saturday. On Friday and Sunday, you are entitled to 25 percent off. Simply present proof of your age when you buy your tickets. You will also get a discount on Voyageur's one-day bus or riverboat tours out of such major cities as Montreal, Ottawa, and Toronto.

A deal that may profit you even more than your senior discount, however, if you plan extensive travel in these provinces, is the TourPass that is available to all ages and may be used from May 1 through October 31. Check it out.

For information: Voyageur Colonial Ltd., 505 De Maisonneuve Blvd. East, 3rd floor, Montreal, Quebec, Canada H2L 1Y4; 514-842-2281 in Montreal; 416-393-7911 in Toronto.

ONTARIO NORTHLAND

An excursion railroad that takes you on wilderness tours of Canada's north country through areas accessible only by rail or plane, Ontario Northland offers travelers 65 or older a 50 percent fare reduction any day of the year. Although it does not apply to package tours, it may be used for other travel on the line, including the Polar Bear Express, an excursion from Cochrane to Moosonee, near James Bay, that operates from mid-June until Labor Day.

For information: Ontario Northland, 65 Front St. West, Toronto, ON M5J 1E6, Canada; in Ontario and Quebec, 1-800-268-9281; elsewhere, 416-965-4268.

GO BY BOAT

Alaska Marine Highway

On this line's coastal ferries in the winter season—October 1 through April 30—passengers who are 65 or older sail for half of the normal fare within Alaskan waters. That means you must be leaving from an Alaskan port and landing at an Alaskan port. Or, if you are willing to go standby, space available, you pay only a $5 fee for each leg of your trip, making a reservation on the day of sailing at the terminal.

For information: Call 1-800-642-0066.

Chapter Ten
Hotels and Motels: Get Your Over-50 Markdowns

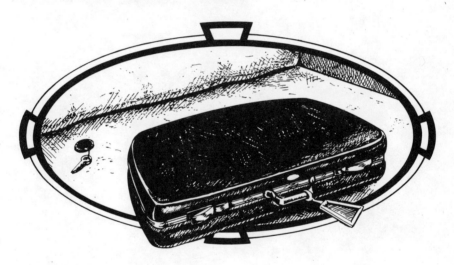

Across the United States and Canada, major chains of hotels and motels (and individual establishments as well) are chasing the mature market—that's you. As a candidate for an increasing barrage of bargains in lodgings, you may not have to sell all the family jewels to afford your next trip.

To get your discounts at most establishments, all that's required is evidence that you are 55, or 60, or 65, as the case may be. Or that you are a member of a club that makes many of the same savings available to you at 50. When you join AARP or a similar organization, you will receive a list of the lodging chains that offer special rates to reward you for having lived so long.

But, first, keep in mind:

If you want to take advantage of the discounts coming to you, be sure to do some advance scouting and planning with your travel agent or on your own.

▶ In this rapidly changing world, rates and policies can be altered in a flash, so an update is always advisable.
▶ Information about discounts is seldom volunteered. In most cases, you must arrange for them when you make your reservations and remind the desk clerk of them again when you check in. Do not wait until you're settling your bill because then it may be too late.

▶ Usually, over-50 discounts are subject to "space availability." That means it may be pretty hard to get them when you want to travel. So always book early, demanding your discount privileges, and try to be flexible on your dates in order to take advantage of them. Your best bets for space are usually weekends in large cities, weekdays at resorts, and non–holiday seasons.

▶ It's quite possible that a special promotional rate, especially in off-peak seasons or on weekends, may save you more money than your senior discount. Many hotels, especially in big cities and warm climates, cut their prices drastically in the summer, for example. Others that cater mostly to business people during the week try to encourage weekend traffic by offering bargain rates if you stay over a Saturday night. Resorts are often eager to fill their rooms on weekdays. So always investigate all the possibilities before you get too enthusiastic about using your hard-earned senior discount, and remember to ask for the *lowest available rate.*

▶ There are several chains of no-frills budget motels that don't offer discounts or too much in the way of amenities but do charge very low room rates and tend to be located along the most-traveled routes.

▶ In most cases, not every hotel or inn in a chain will offer the discount. Those that do are called "participating" hotels/motels.

▶ In addition to the chains, many individual hotels and inns are eager for your business and offer special reduced rates. Always *ask* before making a reservation. Your travel agent should be able to help you with this.

▶ Some hotel restaurants will give you a discount too, usually whether or not you are a registered guest.

▶ By the way, your discount will not be given on top of other special discounts. One discount is all you get.

ASTON HOTELS AND RESORTS
Aston's Sun Club gives you at age 55—and your traveling companions—a discount of about 20 percent on the room rates at its hotels and condominium resorts in Hawaii and California. Sometimes it also throws in a free subcompact rental car and gifts. Ask for the special rates and other offerings when you reserve your room and take proof of your age with you when you check in. Sun Club rooms are limited in number, so reserve early.
For information: Call 1-800-922-7866.

BEST WESTERN
This huge chain of independently owned motels offers a 10 percent discount on the room rates to people over 55 years of age at almost all of its properties in the United States and Canada. If you belong to AARP, you get the discount at 50. Advance reservations are required, and so is proof of age when you check in.
For information: Call 1-800-528-1234.

BUDGETEL INNS
Budgetel Inns are inexpensive motels located in 20 states, mostly in the South and Midwest. About half of them will give you a 10 percent discount if you are 55 years old, so check this out when you make your reservations.
For information: Call 1-800-428-3438.

CALINDA QUALITY INNS
These hotels, part of the Choice Hotels International chain, in 13 locations in Mexico take 30 percent off the room rates and, in most locations, 15 percent off food

and beverages for members of AARP and other senior organizations. But rooms at this rate are limited, so reserve early. You must guarantee your reservation with a major credit card and cancel by 6 P.M. on the day of your arrival. An alternative plan is the Prime Time program that gives AARP members at 50 and anyone over 60 an uncomplicated 10 percent discount.
For information: Call 1-800-228-5151.

CHOICE HOTELS
Choice Hotels International—which includes Quality Inns, Comfort Inns, Clarion Hotels and Resorts, Calinda Quality Inns, Friendship Inns, Econo Lodges, Rodeway Inns, and Sleep Inns—operates more than 2,000 hotels worldwide. Most of them offer their Prime Time program, which gives 10 percent off the room rates any day of the year to guests who are 60 years old or members of AARP, CARP, United's Silver Wings Plus, or other senior organizations. The discount applies to the company's all-suite hotels as well as hotels and motels.

Even better, you can get a 30 percent reduction in rates at participating inns if you plan ahead. This Senior Saver rate is yours when you make your reservation early and guarantee it with a major credit card.
For information: Call 1-800-221-2222.

CLARION HOTELS AND RESORTS
See Choice Hotels.

COLONY HOTELS AND RESORTS
You will get a 25 percent discount here if you belong to AARP or 20 percent otherwise simply because you are over 60. These hotels are located on five Hawaiian islands and in nine mainland states.
For information: Call 1-800-777-1700.

COMFORT INNS
See Choice Hotels.

CONRAD HOTELS
The international subsidiary of Hilton USA, Conrad Hotels in Europe, Australia, Mexico, Hong Kong, and the Caribbean participate in Hilton's Senior HHonors Program for over-60s. Members of the club are entitled to 25 to 50 percent off room rates. For more, see Hilton Hotels.

COUNTRY HEARTH INNS
A string of moderate-cost motels, Country Hearth Inns take 10 percent off the room rate if you can prove you're over 50 years of age.
For information: Call 1-800-848-5767 or, in Ohio, 1-800-282-5711.

COUNTRY INN COLLECTION
This is a group of charming and picturesque country inns sprinkled throughout New England. All offer a discount of 10 percent on room rates to visitors over 60. Most of the inns are in restored historic buildings and offer beautiful scenery, good food, and hospitality.
For information: Call 1-800-852-4667.

COURTYARD BY MARRIOTT
Here AARP members are in luck—they get 15 percent discount off the regular room rates as well as 15 percent off lunch and dinner (food and nonalcoholic beverages) at the hotel restaurants whether they are hotel guests or not. Nonmembers must be 62 to get a 10 percent discount on lodging.
For information: Call 1-800-321-2211.

CROWNE PLAZA HOTELS
See Holiday Inns.

DAYS INNS, HOTELS, SUITES, AND DAY STOPS
One of the largest lodging chains in this country and abroad, Days Inns invites you at age 50 to join its September Days Club, entitling you to 15 percent to 40 percent off rooms at about 1,000 participating hotels, motels, suites, and lodges. You also get 10 percent off your meals at participating Days Inns restaurants and your purchases at its gift shops, discounts on rental cars, discounts on prescription and over-the-counter drugs, discounts on entertainment attractions and theme parks, trips and escorted tours at group rates, information on last-minute travel bargains, a quarterly travel magazine, and a lot more perks. Membership costs $12 a year for you and your spouse. Most inns also give AARP members 10 percent off on rooms.
For information: Call 1-800-241-5050.

DORAL HOTELS
Doral's Classics Club, for people over the age of 60, gives you accommodations at bargain rates at any of the four Doral hotels in Manhattan—Doral Court, Doral Inn, Doral Park Avenue, and Doral Tuscany. At this writing, the club offers a one-bedroom suite at $150 per room/ per night or a deluxe room at $110, subject to availability. A continental breakfast is included, as is free parking on Friday or Saturday nights at three of the hotels. The club's concierge will assist with reservations, tickets, and transportation.
For information: Call 1-800-22-DORAL.

DOUBLETREE CLUB HOTELS

If you are 60—or 50 and a member of a recognized senior organization—you will get about 15 percent off the room rates at these hotels scattered around the U.S. and Canada. Breakfast, cocktails, and late-night snacks are included.

For information: Call 1-800-426-6774.

DOUBLETREE HOTELS

These luxury hotels, concentrated in the West, give Silver Leaf discounts of about 15 percent to travelers who are 60 or older (or are members of AARP), but each determines its own policy, so you'll have to check the specific hotel that interests you to find out what it offers.

For information: Call 1-800-528-0444.

DOWNTOWNER MOTOR INNS

See Red Carpet Inns.

DRURY INNS

These budget motels offer a 10 percent discount on the regular room rates at all of their 41 locations to anyone 50 or over. Just ask and have your proof of age handy.

For information: Call 1-800-325-8300.

ECONO LODGES

See Choice Hotels.

ECONOMY INNS OF AMERICA

This economy lodging chain, with motels located near major highways in California, Florida, South Carolina,

and Georgia, gives 10 percent off the already low room rates to AARP members and anyone over 55. Just ask for it.
For information: Call 1-800-826-0778.

EMBASSY SUITES
These classy hotels feature two-room suites with free breakfast and complimentary cocktails and take up to 10 percent off the regular room rates for members of AARP, the National Retired Teachers Association, and the National Council of Senior Citizens. That is, if they are participating in the program. If you're not a cardholder, you'll get the discount anyway at most of the hotels just for being over 65—in some cases, only 55.
For information: Call 1-800-362-2779.

FAIRFIELD INNS BY MARRIOTT
At Marriott's economy lodging chain, you will get 10 percent deducted from your bill if you are over 62. And you're entitled to a 15 percent deduction (except during special events) if you belong to AARP.
For information: Call 1-800-228-2800.

FRIENDSHIP INNS
See Choice Hotels.

GUEST QUARTERS
A small chain with about 30 locations and one- and two-bedroom suites only, Guest Quarters takes off 10 percent or more for members of AARP at most of its hotels.
For information: Call 1-800-424-2900.

HAMPTON INNS

The LifeStyle 50 program offers a four-for-one deal for people over 50. This means a guest may share a double room with three other adults over 50 at any of the 216 Hampton Inns around the country and pay only the single rate. Free continental breakfasts come with the room. Simply show proof that you are over 50 when you check in and sign up for a free LifeStyle 50 membership card there and then. Or you may get an application by calling the number below.

For information: Call 1-800-HAMPTON.

HARLEY HOTELS

Look for a 10 percent discount at all of these hotels—except those in New York City—simply by flashing your AARP or other senior organization card.

For information: Call 1-800-321-2323.

HILTON HOTELS

Hilton's Senior HHonors Travel Club is an excellent deal for you if you're 60 years old. As a member you are entitled to 25 to 50 percent off the room rates at 250 participating Hilton Hotels in the United States and 80 Hilton and Conrad Hotels in 39 countries. You also get 20 percent off the bill on dinner for two at 260 participating hotel restaurants in the U.S. and Canada, whether or not you are a hotel guest.

The Senior HHonors room rates are also available to your children, parents, or grandchildren who are traveling with you and are guaranteed to be the lowest published rates offered. Membership costs $35 a year for you and your spouse for use in the United States or $50 a year to save at Hilton Hotels worldwide ($200 for life worldwide) and includes your spouse. You must enroll in the club before booking a trip with the discount.

For those who can't join the Senior HHonors Travel Club but do belong to AARP, many of the hotels offer a 10 percent discount off regular room rates.
For information: Call 1-800-445-8667.

HOLIDAY INN
Your best bet here is to join Holiday's Preferred Senior Traveler Program because members of this free club for people over 50 get room rates reduced by 20 percent at participating Holiday Inn Hotels, Crowne Plaza Hotels, and Holiday Inn Express, worldwide. Not only that, but members also have 10 percent deducted from their food bills at any of the hotel restaurants whether they are staying at the inn or just dropping by for a meal. Members of recognized senior organizations get a discount on room rates (10 percent in most cases). Ask for it when you make your reservations and again at check-in.
For information: Call 1-800-HOLIDAY.

HOWARD JOHNSON
Howard Johnson Road Rally, a special program for people 60-plus and for over-50 card-carrying members of AARP, CARP, or other recognized senior organizations, offers up to 30 percent off regular room rates. To get the 30 percent discount you must make advanced reservations, because the number of rooms available at this rate are limited at some times of the year. But you can always get at least a 15 percent reduction on the regular rates simply by checking into a participating HJ and showing your ID.
For information: Call 1-800-634-3464.

HYATT HOTELS AND RESORTS
Hyatt Hotels and Resorts in the U.S., Canada, and the Caribbean offer a discount of about 25 percent off the regular room rates (each hotel has its own policy) to travelers 55 or over. Simply ask for it when you make your reservations. The senior rate is subject to availability so, especially during peak travel periods, be sure to reserve early.
For information: Call 1-800-228-9000.

INN SUITES
With seven inns in Arizona and California, this small chain will give you—at age 65, or 50 with an AARP card—a 10 percent discount on regular room rates on its one- and two-room suites. Included is complimentary breakfast, a morning newspaper, and a free cocktail hour.
For information: Call 1-800-842-4242.

JOURNEY'S END HOTELS, MOTELS, SUITES
You are entitled to a 10 percent discount off the regular rates if you belong to AARP, CARP, or are 55 (60 in Canada) at any of about 130 locations in Canada and the northeastern U.S.
For information: Call 1-800-668-4200.

KNIGHTS INNS/ARBORGATE INNS
This budget motel chain with about 160 locations mostly in the Southeast gives a discount of 10 percent throughout the year to anyone over 55.
For information: Call 1-800-722-7220.

LA QUINTA MOTOR INNS
With about 200 locations mostly in the Sunbelt, these motor inns are inexpensive and become even more so when you ask for your 10 percent discount. You'll get it if you are a member of AARP or a similar organization or if you are 55 and can prove it. It is sometimes not available during special events in some locations. La Quinta also offers its Senior Class program for people over 60. For a one-time $10 membership fee, you are entitled to 20 percent off the room rate plus some other incidental benefits. Apply at any hotel in the chain or write Senior Class, PO Box 27128, Minneapolis, MN 55427.
For information: Call 1-800-531-5900.

L&K MOTELS
A budget chain in middle America, L&K takes 15 percent off for AARP members and anybody else over 55.
For information: Call 1-800-282-5711.

MARRIOTT HOTELS, RESORTS, AND SUITES
Marriott's program for over-50s is among the best deals around if you are a member of AARP or CARP and can plan ahead. With an AARP or CARP membership card and a 21-day nonrefundable advance booking, you will get at least 50 percent off the regular rate at almost 200 participating locations. You must pay in advance for the entire stay by check or credit card when you make your reservation.

For those who can't commit themselves three weeks ahead, there is an automatic 10 percent discount on regular room rates every day of the year for AARP or CARP card carriers.

Both discounts apply to additional rooms, if they are

available, so family members or friends traveling with you can share your good fortune.

There is also a 25 percent discount on meals (except on specials and alcoholic beverages) at most of the hotels and resorts for your party of up to eight people. This may be used as often as you like, and you are not required to be an overnight guest to get this restaurant discount, but you must present your AARP card. Always ask first if the hotel or resort is participating in the discount plan.

And more: you'll get a 10 percent discount on gift-shop purchases at any of Marriott's hotels and resorts, except for certain items such as tobacco and candy.

One hitch: the room discounts may not be available at all times, especially during peak periods.
For information: Call 1-800-228-9290.

MASTER HOSTS INNS
See Red Carpet Inns.

NENDELS MOTOR INNS
A Pacific Northwest chain of inns, Nendels takes about 10 percent off the regular room rates at most of its locations for members of all senior organizations and those over 65. The discount is also available at Value Inns by Nendels. Ask for it when you make your reservation or check in.
For information: Call 1-800-547-0106.

OMNI HOTELS
Omni Hotels are another winner in this series. The participating hotels in this group—almost 40 of them in the United States and Mexico—offer AARP members a 50

percent discount on regular room rates, based on space availability. You'll also get a 15 percent discount on food and nonalcoholic beverages in some of their restaurants if you are a registered hotel guest. To receive the special room rate, reserve ahead, request the discount. At check-in you will be asked to show your AARP membership card. In the restaurants, present it before you place your order.

For information: Call 1-800-THE-OMNI.

OUTRIGGER HOTELS HAWAII

With hotels all over the islands, Outrigger's Fifty Plus package offers you a 20 percent discount off the regular room rates on all rooms at all times. For members of AARP, the discount is even more—25 percent. The discounts are yours for the asking.

For information: Call 1-800-733-7777.

PASSPORT INNS

See Red Carpet Inns.

QUALITY INNS

See Choice Hotels.

RADISSON HOTELS

Radisson will give you and family members traveling with you a discount of 10 to 25 percent on regular rates at all of its locations worldwide, based on availability. To get the lower rate at some hotels you must have reached your 62nd birthday and make advance reservations. At others, you get it at 50 or 55. Mention the discount when you reserve the room and again when you check in.

For information: Call 1-800-333-3333.

RAMADA INTERNATIONAL HOTELS AND RESORTS

Ramada's Best Years Program is an excellent deal for you if you belong to any of a long list of senior organizations, including the over-50 clubs, or are 60 years old. It entitles you to 25 percent off the regular rates on any available room at most of Ramada's establishments in the U.S., as well as 35 other countries, including the Caribbean. Grandchildren may stay free if they share your room. There may be blackout periods, so reserve ahead.

For information: Call 1-800-272-6232.

RED CARPET INNS

Red Carpet Inns, Master Hosts Inns, Passport Inns, Downtowner Motor Inns and Scottish Inns are all operated by Hospitality International, and almost all of them in the United States and Canada give AARP members or anybody else who's 55 a 10 percent discount on room rates year-round, except perhaps during special local events, when available rooms are very scarce.

For information: Call 1-800-251-1962.

RED LION HOTELS AND INNS

To over-50s who present AARP or Mature Outlook cards, Red Lions and Thunderbirds—all in the western states—give their Prime Rate, which amounts to 20 percent off the regular room rates. Book ahead, because there are occasional blackout periods. In addition, some of their restaurants give you 10 percent off food chosen from the regular menu, except on holidays.

For information: Call 1-800-547-8010.

RED ROOF INNS

Red Roof Inns, a large economy lodging chain with over 200 locations in 30 states, offers a program called RediCard +60. For a $10 fee, plus $2 for a spouse, you may join the program at age 60, entitling you to a 10 percent discount on room rates, plus three coupons worth $5 each that are valid at any Red Roof Inn, a road map in its own travel pouch, a quarterly newsletter, and other privileges.
For information: Call 1-800-843-7663.

RELAX INNS AND HOTELS

Located in Canada, these 26 hotels will give anyone over the age of 55 a 15 percent discount off the regular room rate. If you join their free Club 55 Plus, you'll be entitled to the discount and, in addition, one night free after five nights at any of the inns or hotels. The nights need not be consecutive.
For information: Call 1-800-66-RELAX.

RESIDENCE INNS BY MARRIOTT

Participating inns in this chain of all-suite accommodations designed for extended stays offer a 15 percent discount or more on the rates to members of AARP or people over the age of 58.
For information: Call 1-800-331-3131.

SANDMAN HOTELS AND INNS

All situated in western Canada, these 20 inns take about 25 percent off the regular room rate if you are 55 or over. Write in advance for a Club 55 Card: 1755 W. Broadway, Suite 310, Vancouver, BC V6J 4S5, Canada.
For information: Call 1-800-663-6900.

SCOTTISH INNS

See Red Carpet Inns.

SHERATON HOTELS

Sheraton's hundreds of establishments all over the world give AARP members at 50 or anybody else at 60 a good break: a 25 percent discount on all but the minimum room rates. You'll need advance reservations and proper identification. The discount may not be available at peak periods. Grandchildren stay free in your room.
For information: Call 1-800-325-3535.

SHONEY'S INNS

These inexpensive motels, about 60 of them, are concentrated in the Southeast and Midwest. Here, if you join the Merit Club 50 at age 50 or older, you will receive the single-person rate for up to four people in a room. Traveling alone? You get discounts that vary from inn to inn. Always ask for them. Sign up for the club at an inn or over the telephone when you make your reservations.
For information: Call 1-800-222-2222.

SLEEP INNS

See Choice Hotels.

SONESTA INTERNATIONAL HOTELS

This collection of 15 luxury hotels gives members of AARP a 10 percent discount at three of its establishments and a 15 percent discount at six others, including those in New Orleans and Bermuda. Request your special rate when you make your reservations in advance.
For information: Call 1-800-766-3782.

STOUFFER HOTELS

Stouffer's Great Years program gives guests over 60 a room for about half the regular rate, single or double occupancy. In one hotel, for example, the regular room rate is $190 (double) at this writing, while the Great Years rate is $63, so this is an opportunity worth considering. Advance reservations are required, rooms are limited to availability, and the special rate does not apply to some Stouffer resorts. It's good any day of the week, year-round. Some Stouffer Hotels also honor the AARP card with a discount.

For information: Call 1-800-HOTELS-1.

SUPER 8 MOTELS

Many of the over 800 no-frills budget motels in this chain give a 10 percent discount to members of over-50 clubs or people "over a certain age," that age differing according to the location.

For information: Call 1-800-843-1991.

THUNDERBIRD MOTOR INNS

See Red Lion Inns.

TRAVELODGE

Travelodge, a division of Forte Hotels, offers an unrestricted 15 percent discount on room rates at over 500 properties to anyone 50 and over who joins its Classic Travel Club. The free membership also offers a discount on some car rentals, a quarterly newsletter with other savings and coupons, room upgrades at some hotels, free morning coffee, and instant enrollment via a toll-free hotline.

Members of AARP and CARP will get the 15 percent discount but not the additional privileges.

For information: To enroll in the Classic Travel Club, call 1-800-545-6343. For reservations, call 1-800-526-2582.

VAGABOND INNS
Concentrated on the West Coast, this group of 39 inns has its Club 55 for mature travelers who are at least— three guesses—55! The club offers a special rate that gives you 10 to 20 percent off the regular single room rate. Not only that, but one to four adults may stay in your double room (with two double beds) at no extra charge at most of the hotels. Club membership costs nothing and gets you $10 in coupons good toward a stay at any Vagabond Inn and a quarterly newsletter outlining special senior travel events in the area. Join up at a Vagabond Inn, on the telephone (toll-free number below), or by writing to the club for an application. Another perk here is the Tenth Night program, which gives you a free night after you have racked up nine nights at any Vagabond Inns.
For information: Call 1-800-522-1555 or write to The Vagabond Inns Club 55, Box 85011, San Diego, CA 92186-5011.

VISCOUNT HOTELS
Because these hotels are affiliated with Travelodge, you are entitled to a 15 percent discount and special privileges if you are 50 and belong to the free Classic Travel Club (see Travelodge). Members of AARP also get a 15 percent savings on room rates.
For information: To enroll in the Classic Travel Club, call 1-800-545-6343. For reservations, call 1-800-526-2582.

WESTIN HOTELS AND RESORTS
These luxury hotels often offer senior rates (often up to 50 percent off regular prices), but each has its own policy, so always ask about the possibilities when you

make your reservations. Where there is no senior discount, ask for the weekend rate, usually 50 percent off, or the corporate rate, 20 to 25 percent off. All of these special rates, of course, are based on availability. If you belong to United Airlines Silver Wings Plus and rooms are available, you'll get a 50 percent reduction.
For information: Call 1-800-228-3000.

GOOD DEALS IN RESTAURANTS

Many restaurants offer discounts to people in their prime, but in most cases you'll have to seek them out yourself, by asking or watching the ads in your local newspaper. In addition, a few large hotel chains will give you a break on your food bills when you eat in their restaurants. For example:

At **Hilton Hotels** restaurants in the U.S., you're entitled to a 20 percent discount on dinners for two, hotel guests or not, if you are a member of Hilton's Senior HHonors travel club.

Holiday Inn restaurants give a discount of 10 percent off your check when you dine there if you belong to Holiday's Preferred Senior Traveler Program (See pages 115–116).

The restaurants in the participating **Marriott Hotels and Resorts** will take 25 percent off your bill for a party of up to eight people if you belong to AARP, whether or not you are staying at the hotel.

At **Omni Hotels** you'll get 15 percent taken off the check for food and nonalcoholic beverages in the hotel restaurants by flashing your AARP card. The discount is yours at any hour if you are staying at the hotel, but only before 7 P.M. if you are not.

The restaurants at **Red Lion Inns** and **Thunderbird Motor Inns** will reduce your food bill by 15 percent on regular-priced items if you belong to AARP. Be ready to produce your membership card.

Chapter Eleven
Alternative Lodgings for Thrifty Wanderers

I f you're willing to be innovative, imaginative, and occasionally fairly spartan, you can travel for a song or thereabouts. Here are some novel lodgings that can save you money and, at the same time, supply you with adventures worth talking about for years. They are not all designed specifically for people over 50, but each reports that a good portion of its clientele consists of free spirits of a certain age who are looking to beat the high cost of travel, meet people from other places, and have a real good time.

For more ways to cut travel costs and get smart in the bargain, check out the residential/educational programs in Chapter 16.

BIG APPLE ON A BUDGET

For visitors to New York City who do not wish to run up big hotel bills, inexpensive dormitory rooms are available in Hoboken, New Jersey, just across the river at Stephens Institute of Technology, 10 minutes by 24-hour bus to the big city. The rooms are even less expensive for people over 50 who mention this book. Rooms are limited during the school year, but many are available in the summer.

For information: Campus Holidays USA, 242 Bellevue Ave., Upper Montclair, NJ 07043; 1-800-526-2915.

CAMPUS TRAVEL SERVICE

More than 700 colleges and universities in the United States, Canada, New Zealand, Australia, and Europe open their dormitories to travelers every summer. They offer spartan but adequate student rooms at bargain prices—an average of $20 a night—plus, in most cases, use of all campus facilities from swimming pool to cafeteria. Some include breakfast or, for not much more, three meals a day. Check with the colleges in the area you want to visit or get a copy of *U.S. and Worldwide Accommodations Guide* for $13 plus $1.50 postage. This lists the campuses offering guest lodgings, the cost, the available dates, meal plans, and information about facilities and activities. The rooms—and occasionally bedroom suites—are usually available by the day, the week, or the month.

For information and the directory: Campus Travel Service, PO Box 8355, Newport Beach, CA 92660; 714-720-3729.

THE EVERGREEN CLUB

This is a bed-and-breakfast club for singles or couples over 50 who have guest rooms in their homes that they're willing to make available to fellow club members traveling through their areas. No matter how elegant or simple your home is, no matter how close or far from the beaten path, the visitors pay $10 per night for single accommodations and $15 for double. You may not get rich on this venture, but you will meet a lot of interesting people. And, in return, you may stay in other people's homes at the same prices when you're on the road.

Organized 10 years ago, the Evergreen Club now includes inexpensive, comfortable accommodations in about 500 homes in the United States and Canada along with a handful abroad and down under.

You pay $50 (per couple) or $40 (single) yearly dues. You'll get a membership card, an annual directory, and quarterly newsletters. The directory gives names and addresses of members, occupations and interests, policies about pets and smoking, and listings of nearby special attractions. Members make their own reservations and arrangements with one another.

For information: Send a self-addressed, stamped envelope to the Evergreen Club, 404 N. Galena Ave., Dixon, IL 61021; 815-288-9600.

INNter LODGING CO-OP

Yet another way of sharing your home with other travelers and parlaying that guest room into virtually free lodging for yourself when you travel in the United States, Canada, and Europe. Guests pay about $5 per adult per night, depending upon whether there are private bathroom facilities. Children, who must arrive with their own sleeping bags, are an extra 25¢ a night. You must make your own arrangements directly with the hosts or the travelers who wish to stay with you.

When you join, you receive a membership card and a directory of participating hosts. Anyone any age may join, but the plan tends to appeal most to young families and mature travelers.

For information: INNter Lodging Co-op Services, PO Box 7044, Tacoma, WA 98407-0044; 206-756-0343.

NEW PALTZ SUMMER LIVING

Consider spending a couple of the hottest months in the mountains, about 75 miles north of New York City. Every summer, while the usual student occupants are on vacation, 204 furnished garden apartments are reserved for seniors in the village of New Paltz, home of the State University of New York at New Paltz. The rents at this writing for the entire summer (from early June until late August) range from $1,900 to $3,500, depending on the size of the apartment. Living right in town next to the campus, you may audit college courses free and attend lectures and cultural events. There are two heated pools and a tennis court in the complex, as well as a clubhouse. Buses travel to New York every Wednesday for those who want to go to the theater, and there are frequent day trips to other places of interest.

For information: New Paltz Summer Living, 19 E. Colonial Dr., New Paltz, NY 12561; 914-255-7205.

OAKWOOD RESORT APARTMENTS

Travelers over 55 may rent apartments in several states at a 25 percent discount during the winter months, choosing among locations in California, Texas, Virginia, Las Vegas, Chicago, Detroit, Philadelphia, Memphis, and Denver. You must rent for 30 days or longer from November 1 through the end of April to get the discount. All of the Oakwood Resort Apartments have kitchens and come completely furnished and equipped with TV, dishes, pots and pans, and linens. Weekly maid service and utilities are included. Most locations also have swimming pools, tennis courts, party rooms, and fitness centers.

For information: Oakwood Resort Apartments, R&B Enterprises, 2222 Corinth Ave., Los Angeles, CA 90064; 1-800-888-0103.

SENIOR VACATION HOTELS OF FLORIDA

These hotels take a novel approach, with two-week minimum vacation packages year-round at four different hotels for seniors only (in Bradenton, Lakeland, and St. Petersburg). These are all-inclusive, with two meals, transportation, excursions, boat trips, entertainment, parties, and activities in the bundle. Current rates start at $850 (single) and $700 (per person, double) for a month in November, December, and April; more in January, February, or March. While the hotels will certainly accept you at age 50, you'll fit into the group more snugly if you're a bit more than that.

For information: Senior Vacation Hotels of Florida, 7401 Central Ave., St. Petersburg, FL 33710; 1-800-247-2203 (in Canada, 1-800-843-3713).

SENIORS ABROAD

Seniors Abroad is an international home-stay program exclusively for travelers over 50, offering an opportunity to stay in homes in other countries and learn firsthand how other people live. You pay your own costs which are reasonable because you have no hotel bills and many of your meals are home-cooked. Going overseas in escorted groups of 20 to 30 singles and couples, you spend three weeks in the country of your choice—Japan, Australia, New Zealand, Denmark, Sweden, or Norway—for three consecutive stays of a week each with native hosts who are also over 50. Orientation, sight-seeing, and visits to U.S. embassies are included. You may also play host to foreign travelers visiting this country.

For information: Contact Evelyn Zivetz, Seniors Abroad, 12533 Pacato Circle North, San Diego, CA 92128; 619-485-1696.

SERVAS

Servas is "an international cooperative system of hosts and travelers established to help build world peace, goodwill, and understanding . . . among people of diverse cultures and backgrounds." A nonprofit, nongovernmental, interracial, and interfaith organization open to all ages, it provides lists of hosts, along with their activities and interests, all over the United States as well as the rest of the world. You make your own arrangements to stay with them, usually for two days, and share their everyday lives and concerns. No money changes hands. The hospitable people who take you in do this so they may enjoy your company and learn about you and your culture. You do the same for other travelers in return. There is a membership fee of $45 per year and you will be asked for two letters of reference and an interview.

For information: Send a #10 self-addressed, stamped envelope to US Servas, 11 John St., New York, NY 10038; 212-267-0252.

SUN CITY CENTER

Between Tampa and Sarasota in Florida, Sun City Center wants you to discover what a large self-contained retirement town is all about and offers a vacation package as a sample of life there. You may vacation here for four days (three nights), seven days, or three days. At this writing, a stay of four days, three nights, per couple, with daily continental breakfast, two rounds of golf each, tennis, swimming, and club facilities, costs $90 from April 15 to September 30; $190 from October 1 to January 15; and $229 from February 1 to April 14.

For information: Sunmark Communities, PO Box 5698, Sun City Center, FL 33570; 1-800-237-8200 (in Florida, 1-800-282-8040).

SUN CITY WEST, SUN CITY TUCSON, AND SUN CITY LAS VEGAS

All three of these related retirement communities offer inexpensive vacation stays designed to give you a taste of what goes on in such a place and, of course, to persuade you to pack up and move there. One of a visiting two-some must be 55 years old and neither of you may be under 19 to take advantage of the offer.

Sun City West, with about 18,000 residents, is located 30 miles outside of Phoenix. Here the vacation special gives two people a week in a furnished garden apartment, the use of the facilities, including seven 18-hole golf courses, and a tour. At this writing you pay, per couple, $199 plus tax June through October; $299 November through January; and $450 February through March. And there are even cheaper specials offered throughout the year.

Sun City Tucson, eight miles north of the city at the foot of the Catalina Mountains, is a smaller version planned for 5,000 residents, with a desert golf course. Current rates: $199 plus tax per couple in June, July, and August; $299 in May and September through December; and $450 January through April.

Sun City Las Vegas, 12 miles out of the city, puts two of you up at Marriott's Residence Inn, a block from The Strip, for three nights and four days for $239 to introduce you to the community. Here the perks are a free round of golf and lunch for two, a daily continental breakfast, a hospitality hour weekday evenings, your own kitchen, and airport shuttle.

For information: Sun City West: 1-800-528-2604. Sun City Tucson: 1-800-433-9611. Sun City Las Vegas: 1-800-843-4848.

TRAVELCLUB BED & BREAKFAST

This bed-and-breakfast club, an offshoot of the Evergreen Club (see pages 130–131), is similar to its mother organization, but its more than 200 members throughout the United States are over-50s who want to know where to find inexpensive B&B lodgings in other people's homes without having to play host to other travelers in return. Current overnight rates: $18 single, $24 double, including breakfast. Yearly club membership costs $40 for a single person, $50 for a couple. You will receive a host directory, updates, and a newsletter and make your own arrangements

For information: Send a stamped self-addressed business-size envelope to TravelClub, 404 N. Galena Ave., Dixon, IL 61021; 815-288-9600.

UNIVERSITY BRITAIN

A traveler any age, including yours, gets bed and full English breakfast for $40 to $50 per person ($36 to $45 if you mention this book) in a residence hall of King's College, in London. Or you may choose to stay in any of eight campus locations in Scotland. The rooms are available during July, August, and September as well as during other vacation periods. You may stay for as many nights as you wish, usually in a single room, but sometimes twin rooms are available.

Other alternative lodgings offered by this agency are studio apartments located in central London. At the Royal Court, you'll get a double studio for $135 per night at this writing (with a 10 percent discount if you're over 50 and mention this book). The apartments are available any time of the year.

For information: Campus Holidays USA, 242 Bellevue Ave., Upper Montclair, NJ 07043; 1-800-526-2915.

Chapter Twelve

Perks in Parks and Other Good News

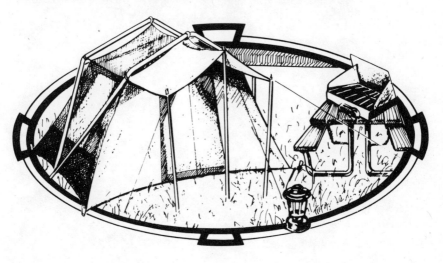

Here and there throughout the United States and Canada, clever states, provinces, and cities have thought up some enticing ideas designed to capture the imagination of people on the other side of 50. Often they are expressing their appreciation of our many contributions to society and simply want to do something nice for us. And sometimes they are trying to lure a few of our vacation dollars to their vicinity, having discovered that we're always out for a good time and know a nice deal when we see one.

But, first, keep in mind:

▶ Before you set forth to visit a new state, it's a good idea to write ahead for free maps, calendars of events, booklets describing sites and scenes of interest, accommodation guides, and perhaps even a list of special discounts or other good things that are available to you as a person in your prime.

▶ Many states offer passes to their state parks and recreation facilities free or at reduced prices to people who are old enough to have learned how to treat them properly.

After the section on national parks, state park passes and other notable deals are described under each state on the following pages. There may be other good deals that have escaped our attention, but those in this chapter are probably the cream of the crop.

ESCAPEES CLUB

Escapees is a club dedicated to providing a support network for RVers, most of whom are on the far side of 50. It publishes a bimonthly newsletter filled with useful information to travelers who carry their homes with them and organizes rallies and retreats around the country as well as seminars on RV living. Other benefits include vehicle insurance, co-op RV parks, a national campground, and mail/message services. Annual membership fee at this writing is $40 a year.
For information: Escapees Inc., Route 5, Box 310, Livingston, TX 77351; 409-327-8873.

NATIONAL PARKS

GOLDEN AGE PASSPORT

Available to anyone over 62, this is a free lifetime entrance permit to all of the federal government's parks, monuments, and recreation areas that charge entrance fees. Anybody who accompanies you in the same non-commercial vehicle also gets in free. If you turn up at the gate in a commercial vehicle such as a bus, the passport admits you and your spouse, your children, and your parents too, so remember to take them along.

You will also get a 50 percent discount on federal use fees charged for facilities and services such as camping, boat launching, parking, cave tours, etc.

The passport is not available by mail. You must pick one up in person at any National Park System area where entrance fees are charged or at any National Park Service and Forest Service headquarters or regional office, most ranger station offices, Fish and Wildlife Service offices, or National Wildlife Refuges. You must have proof of age. A driver's license will do just fine.

(The Golden Access Passport provides the same benefits for the disabled of any age. The Golden Eagle Passport, for those under 62, costs $25 per year.)
For information: National Park Service, PO Box 37127, Washington, DC 20013.

CANADIAN NATIONAL PARKS
All you have to do to get free entry for day visits is to show your driver's license and vehicle registration. The same is generally true for provincial parks, with half-price camping fees charged on the weekends.

OFFERINGS FROM THE STATES
For a free listing of all the state tourism offices and their toll-free numbers, send a self-addressed, stamped envelope to Discover America, Travel Industry Association of America, 2 Lafayette Center, 1133 21st St. NW, Washington, DC 20036.

CALIFORNIA
Palm Springs' Super Seniors is a package of programs and activities designed specifically for people over 50. You'll need a valid P.S. Pass (a free pass that gives you a few discounts in Palm Springs and Palm Desert; get yours at the Palm Springs Leisure Center) and a nominal fee to join. With a Super Senior stamp on your P.S. Pass card, you'll be in line for a free T-shirt, free admis-

sion to a film festival, and discounts on dance lessons, riding lessons, theater admission, ice skating, fitness classes, hikes, dances, and yoga.
For information: Greater Palm Springs Convention and Visitors Bureau, 255 N. El Cielo Rd., Palm Springs, CA 92262-6993; 619-323-8272.

COLORADO
The Aspen Leaf Pass entitles Colorado residents 62 and over to free entrance to state parks and free camping on weekdays. The pass costs $10 per year.
For information: Colorado Division of State Parks, 1313 Sherman St., Room 618, Denver CO 80203; 303-866-3437.

CONNECTICUT
Residents of Connecticut who are over 60 get a free lifetime Charter Oak Pass that gets them into state parks and forests plus Gillette Castle, Dinosaur Park, and Quinebaug Valley Hatchery for free. In fact, their whole carload may enter the parks without charge. To get your pass, write to the address below and send along a copy of your Connecticut driver's license.
For information: State of Connecticut Bureau of Parks and Forests, 165 Capitol Ave., Hartford, CT 06106; 203-566-2304.

FLORIDA
There's a very handy list of Greater Fort Lauderdale Super Senior Savers—discounts on attractions and lodgings especially for the mature set—that will make your stay in that area considerably cheaper. Send for it before you go.

For information: Greater Fort Lauderdale Convention and Visitors Bureau, Dept. MS, 200 East Las Olas Blvd., Suite 1500, Fort Lauderdale, FL 33301; 1-800-22-SUNNY, ext. 711, in the U.S.; 1-800-535-4434, ext. 710, in Canada.

INDIANA
The Golden Hoosier Passport admits Indiana residents over the age of 60 and fellow passengers in a private vehicle to all state parks and natural resources without charge. An application for the Passport, which costs $5 a year, is available at state parks or from the Indiana State Parks Department.
For information: Indiana State Parks Dept., 402 W. Washington St., Room 298, Indianapolis, IN 46204; 317-232-4124.

MAINE
Get your Sixty-Five Plus Pass from the Bureau of Parks and Recreation and you (and anyone in your car with you) will be admitted free to day-use areas at state parks and historic sites.
For information: Maine Bureau of Parks and Recreation, State House Station 22, Augusta, ME; 207-289-2211.

MISSOURI
Missouri residents over the age of 60 are entitled to a free Silver Citizen Discount Card that gives them discounts at restaurants, stores, services, pharmacies, and other businesses throughout the state.
For information: Missouri Dept. of Social Services, PO Box 1337, Jefferson City, MO 65102-1337; 1-800-235-5503.

NEW HAMPSHIRE

An annual event, Seniors' Week in Mt. Washington Valley takes place in September just after Labor Day. In the villages of Eaton, Conway, North Conway, Bartlett, and Jackson, in the White Mountains of New Hampshire, you will find 10 to 15 percent discounts at many of the lodging and eating establishments—if you are 60 years old or more. Special activities such as an art auction, films, and tours are added to the usual opportunities for scenery, outlet shopping, rides on restored steam-powered trains, golf, tennis, hiking, and mountaintop views.

For information: Mt. Washington Valley Visitors Bureau, PO Box 2300, North Conway, NH 03860; 603-356-3171.

NEW YORK

Simply by proving you are a New York resident and are over 62 with your driver's license or a non-driver's ID card issued by the Bureau of Motor Vehicles, you will get all the privileges that used to be yours with New York State's Golden Park Pass. You'll have free vehicle access to state parks and recreational facilities, free admission to state historic sites and arboretums, and a 50 percent reduction on some park activity fees such as swimming and golf.

For information: Call 518-474-0456 or your county Office for the Aging.

OHIO

Residents of Ohio who are 60 or over may get a Golden Buckeye Card for the asking. The Card will get them discounts on goods and services from participating businesses throughout the state. Pick up an application at your local bank or library.

For information: Contact your local Golden Buckeye coordinator for sign-up sites or write to Golden Buckeye Program, 50 W. Broad St., Columbus, OH 43266; 614-466-3681.

PENNSYLVANIA

The City of Philadelphia publishes a booklet, "Philadelphia Seniors on the Go," that lists discounts available year-round to mature people in that city, from transportation to hotels, museums, restaurants, and cultural events. Get yours, go places, and save money. Also, the Visitors Center issues its own senior ID card (for 50 and over) called the Ben Pass, although most places accept an AARP card as proof of age.

For information: Philadelphia Visitors Center, 16th and John F. Kennedy Blvd., Philadelphia, PA 19102; 215-636-1666.

TENNESSEE

Travelers over 55 can find bargains in the state of Tennessee every September, generally from Labor Day to the end of the month. The Senior Class gives you discounts of at least 10 percent on hotels and motels, attractions, restaurants, and retail shops. You'll also get 20 percent off on lodging and camping in state parks most of the year and 10 percent from May 1 through Labor Day with a federal Golden Age Passport.

For information: Tennessee Department of Tourist Development, PO Box 23170, Nashville, TN 37202; 615-741-2158.

UTAH

The Silver Card issued by Park City is a summer program of discounts in this old mining town that's known for its great ski mountains. Many restaurants, retailers and attractions participate in giving older visitors discounts on their wares. To go along with the shopping and eating possibilities, Park City also presents a whole schedule of activities designed especially for the mature crowd.

For information: Park City Convention and Visitors Bureau, 1910 Prospector Ave., Park City, UT 84060; 1-800-453-1360 or 801-649-6100.

GOOD SAM CLUB

The Good Sam Club is an international organization of RVers, mentioned here because the vast majority of people in rolling homes is over 50. This club can be very handy and reassuring when you're cruising the country. Among its benefits are 10 percent discounts on fees at thousands of campgrounds and on propane gas, RV parts and accessories. In addition, it offers a lost-key service, lost-pet service, trip routing, mail-forwarding service, telephone-message service, a magazine, caravan gatherings, and campground directories. Probably the most important benefit is the emergency road service available to members because it includes towing for any vehicle, no matter how large. That's hard to get. Also, there are Good Sam travel tours all over the world, many of them "caraventures." And not least, about 2,200 local chapters hold regular outings, meetings, and camp-outs. Membership costs $19 a year per family.

For information: The Good Sam Club, PO Box 500, Agoura, CA 91301; 1-800-234-3450.

VERMONT
Vermont's residents over 60 may purchase a Green Mountain Passport for $2 from their own town clerk. It is good for a lifetime and entitles them to free day-use admission at any Vermont State Park and its programs. Other benefits include discounts on concerts, restaurant meals, prescriptions, etc.

For information: Vermont Dept. of Aging, 103 S. Main St., Waterbury, VT 05676; 802-241-2400.

WASHINGTON, D.C.
The Golden Washingtonian Club is a discount program in the nation's capital for people over 60. With proof of age, both residents and visitors may get discounts from about 1,800 merchants listed in a directory called *Gold Mine*, which is free at many hotels or at the Washington Tourist Information Center. More than 70 hotels offer 10 to 40 percent off regular rates, 80 restaurants take 5 to 20 percent off meals, and many retail stores take 5 to 25 percent off purchases.

For information: D.C. Committee to Promote Washington, 415 12th St. NW, Ste. 312, Washington DC 20004; 202-724-4091.

WEST VIRGINIA
Everybody who turns 60 in West Virginia gets a Golden Mountaineer Discount Card, which entitles the bearer to discounts from more than 3,500 participating merchants and professionals in the state and a few outside of it. If you don't receive a card automatically, you may apply for one. Flash it wherever you go and save a bundle.

For information: West Virginia Commission on Aging, State Capitol Complex, Holly Grove, Charleston, WV 25305; 304-348-3317.

Chapter Thirteen
Good Deals for Good Sports

Real sports never give up their sneakers. If you've been a physically active sort all your life, you're certainly not going to become a couch potato now—especially since you've probably got more time, energy, and maybe funds than you ever had before to enjoy athletic activities and since you may now take advantage of some enticing special privileges and adventures.

The choices outlined here are not for people whose interest in sports is limited to reclining in comfortable armchairs in front of television sets and watching a football game, or settling down on a hard bench in a stadium with a can of beer, yelling, "Come on, team!" They are for peppy people who do the running themselves.

For such activities as skiing, canoeing, hiking, and biking, be sure to check out the courses and trips offered by Elderhostel (page 199).

SPORTING GROUPS

NATIONAL SENIOR SPORTS ASSOCIATION (NSSA)

A nonprofit organization whose purpose is to encourage sports participation among people over 50, NSSA organizes recreational and competitive golf tournaments in this country and abroad. Its four-day domestic golf holidays are scheduled once or twice a month following the sun to courses all over the U.S. Longer golfing trips to Scotland, Ireland, and Mexico occur a few times a year.

Other NSSA activities include bowling trips and cruises. Membership—$25 for one year, $65 for three years, $150 for life—entitles you to participate in the sports events and trips and also gets you a monthly newsletter, discounts on sporting equipment, and names and addresses of members so you can put together a match when traveling on your own.

For information: NSSA, 10560 Main St., Suite 205, Fairfax, VA 22030; 703-385-7540.

MT. ROBSON ADVENTURE HOLIDAYS

Adventurous over-50s are the exclusive participants in this tour operator's special trips that take place several times every summer high in the Canadian Rockies. Among the outings are hiking/canoeing vacations and heli-camping trips, all of which require you to be in good shape, athletic, and game. See Chapter 3 for more details.

For information: Mt. Robson Adventure Holidays, Box 146, Valemount, BC V0E 2Z0, Canada; 604-566-4351.

OUTDOOR ADVENTURES FOR WOMEN OVER 40

Any reader of this book is certainly over 40 and therefore qualifies, if female, for the trips organized by Outdoor Vacations for Women Over 40. Founded in 1983 by Marion Stoddart, an avid outdoorswoman and conservationist who didn't want to hike, bike, camp out, ski, raft, and canoe with women half her age, this organization attracts physically fit adventurers whose ages, to date, have ranged up to 81.

Ms. Stoddart's surveys have found that a little more than half of the participants in her adventure trips are married; about half are employed; the other half are homemakers, retirees, or volunteers. They come from all over the country, though most are from New England, are in good condition, and rate themselves as beginners or intermediates in the activity they're signing up for. They all love the outdoors, or they wouldn't be there.

The trips are led by trained guides and include instruction, lodging, food, transportation. When you're not camping out in tents or under the stars, you'll be staying in first-rate accommodations.

Previous adventures have included a 10-day walking tour in England, a two-week hiking trip in Austria, cross-country skiing in Glacier National Park, hiking and camping in Hawaii, snorkeling off the Baja California coast, sailing in the British Virgin Islands, canoeing in the Adirondacks, and rafting, hiking, and llama trekking in Yellowstone. There are also day trips out of the Boston area, doing such things as animal tracking, orienteering, hiking, cross-country skiing, and canoeing. **For information:** Outdoor Vacations for Women Over 40, PO Box 200, Groton, MA 01450; 508-448-3331.

THE OVER THE HILL GANG

This international club for energetic people on the far side of 50 began as a ski club (three former Colorado ski instructors were looking for company on the slopes; see Chapter 14), but its members can now be found participating in all kinds of athletic endeavors. Its literature states that it is "an organization for active, fun-loving, adventurous, enthusiastic, young-thinking persons. The only catch is, you have to be 50 or over to join." (Spouses may be younger, however.) You don't have to be a super-jock to be a member, but you do have to like action.

Right now, the club has about 3,000 members and 14 Gangs (chapters) coast to coast—Chicago, Eastern (New York/New Jersey), Las Vegas, Los Angeles, Mt. Hood (Oregon), Mt. Rushmore (South Dakota), New England, New Mexico, Orange County (California), Reno, Rocky Mountain, San Diego, Washington D.C., and Wisconsin. Others are in the making. When there's no Gang in your vicinity, you may become a member at large and join in any of the goings-on. These include ski trips, scuba diving, hiking, vacation trips, camping and fishing, ballooning, surfing, canoeing, etc. Each Gang decides on its own activities. Just plain travel is on the agenda too (see Chapter 3).

The annual fee ($37 per single, $60 per couple) for national membership plus chapter dues, if you have a chapter in your area, gives you a news magazine, chapter and national event information and schedules, discounts, and a chance to join the fun.

For information: Over the Hill Gang International, 6635 S. Dayton St., Ste. 220, Englewood, CO 80111; 303-790-2724.

BONUSES FOR BIKERS

Biking is becoming one of America's most popular sports, and people who never dreamed they could go much farther than around the block are now pedaling up to 150 miles in a day. That includes over-the-hill bikers beyond 50 as well as youngsters of 16, 39, or 47. In fact, some tours and clubs in the U.S. and Canada are designed especially for over-50s.

AMERICAN YOUTH HOSTELS BIKE TOURS

Although almost every organized biking tour would be delighted to have you along as long as you are fairly adept at pedaling, there's one outfit that's actively looking for you. That's American Youth Hostels, which despite its name sometimes offers bike trips—among other adventure trips (see Chapter 3)—specifically for people over 50. That doesn't mean, of course, that you're not also invited to pedal along on any other adult AYH tour.

You'll stay at hostels that offer simple dormitory-style accommodations, eat local food, and meet people who enjoy doing the same kinds of things you like to do. Trips are limited to groups of 10; all are escorted by trained leaders and are astonishingly inexpensive.

Recent trips offered by AYH exclusively for the mature crowd include cycling in Cape Cod and Europe, in French Canada, along the St. Lawrence River, and in New York's Finger Lakes region.

AYH membership, which is required, costs $25 per year unless you're over 55, in which case it's only $15.
For information: AYH, Dept 855, PO Box 37613, Washington, DC 20013-7613; 202-783-6161.

BACKROADS BICYCLE TOURING

Backroads, an established West Coast biking tour operator, has recently begun offering Prime-Time Tours, special bike trips for people over 50. This year there are two weekend tours in California's Santa Ynez Valley.

And, of course, you are welcome to join any of the other tours planned for all ages. If you are single, think about one of the 30 bike trips for single travelers in the U.S. and other parts of the world. Trips are rated for Beginners, Energetic Beginners, Intermediates, and Advanced. All tours are led by a guide and accompanied by a van that carries your luggage—and you, if necessary.

For information: Backroads Bicycle Touring, 1516 5th St., Berkeley, CA 94710; 1-800-533-2573 (in California, 415-527-1555).

BICYCLE TOURING FOR WOMEN ONLY

The same agency mentioned earlier, Outdoor Vacations for Women Over 40, includes a few bike trips among its active offerings. Recently, there was a weekend of biking and walking on Cape Cod. In addition, a trip to Acadia National Park (Maine) includes a day of mountain biking, and a Prince Edward Island (Canada) vacation includes two biking days.

For information: Outdoor Vacations for Women Over 40, PO Box 200, Groton, MA 01450; 508-448-3331.

THE CROSS CANADA CYCLE TOUR SOCIETY

This club was formed in 1982 by a group of "senior cyclists," ranging from about 60 to 75, who biked several thousand miles across Canada in 100 days. Since then, the club has sponsored many cycling trips for all ages and gets local members out for 30- to 50-mile rides twice a week. On the long trips, bikers camp out and make many miles a day. Says the society, "Our aim is to stay alive as long as possible," a worthy goal. Membership costs $20 per year single or $30 per family; most members live in British Columbia.

For information: The Cross Canada Cycle Tour Society, 1200 Hornby St., Vancouver, BC V6Z 2E2, Canada.

ELDERHOSTEL'S INTERNATIONAL BICYCLE TOURS

Elderhostel, famous for its educational travel programs on the campuses of colleges and universities, also offers bicycle tours that combine biking 25 to 35 miles a day with lectures by guides who accompany each trip and guests and specialists from other universities. You bike as a group but at your own pace, with regular stops for lectures, site visits, snacking, and relaxing. Bikes are provided, as are breakfast and dinner. Accommodations are in clean, simple, double hotel rooms, most with private baths. A van travels with you to carry the luggage and bike equipment. It will also give you a ride if you think you can't possibly make it up one more hill.

Current trips include 13 days in England's East Anglia, the chateaux country of France, a lovely area of the Netherlands, or along the Danube. The moderate cost covers airfare and just about everything else except lunches.

For information: Elderhostel, 75 Federal St., 3rd Floor, Boston, MA 02110; 617-426-8056.

INTERNATIONAL BICYCLE TOURS

The Fifty Plus Tour run by IBT is planned for people over 50 who are not into pedaling up mountains but love to cycle. The trip goes to Holland in June and takes you on a leisurely pedal along bicycle paths and quiet country roads on flat terrain through farmland and quaint villages. You'll cover only about 30 miles a day, so there is plenty of time for sightseeing, snacking, and shopping stops. Although this is the only tour strictly limited to over-50s, many who qualify as "mature bikers" are found on IBT's other European bike tours too. And, of course, many more sign on for Elderhostel's European bike tours hosted by IBT.

For information: International Bicycle Tours, 7 Champlin Square, PO Box 754, Essex, CT 06426; 203-767-7005.

THE ONTARIO MASTERS CYCLING ASSOCIATION

A biking club with members from all over the Canadian province of Ontario, all of them over 40 and some of them into their high 70s. It is primarily a racing club and organizes 12 events a year within the province, including time trials of 40 and 80 kilometers as well as pursuit and road races of 60 kilometers.

But the club also organizes bike tours for ordinary nonracing persons of both sexes. And you don't even have to be a formal member to join them—just show up at the start and ride. Among its other enticements, there are social get-togethers, a monthly newsletter listing upcoming events, and tips on buying good bikes and finding good meals en route.

For information: Ontario Masters Cycling Association, John Bonfield, 5 Waterloo St., Brantford, Ontario, N3T 3R5, Canada.

THE TANDEM CLUB OF AMERICA

While not strictly for over-50s, the Tandem Club definitely lists many seniors among its more than 4,000 members so we are including it here. Founded in 1976 by a group of tandem enthusiasts, the club sends out a newsletter full of articles and tips about tandems and touring on them, and promotes rallies for owners of the "long bikes." Membership fee is now $10 in the U.S., $13 in Canada.

For information: Tandem Club of America, c/o Boyd and Allison, 35 E. Centennial Dr., Medford, NJ 08055-8138.

WANDERING WHEELS
A program with a Christian orientation, Wandering Wheels runs long-distance bike tours in this country and abroad, including its 40-day Breakaway Coast-to-Coast for people who are "middle age or older." Its literature says, "The program carries a strong Biblical emphasis."
For information: Wandering Wheels, PO Box 207, Upland, IN, 46989; 317-998-7490.

BICYCLE RACING

Now we're leaving recreational pedaling behind and getting into really serious stuff. So, unless you're a dedicated racer who's in terrific shape, feel free to skip this section.

The United States Cycling Federation, part of the U.S. Olympic Committee, is a racing organization that conducts races for members between the ages of 9 and 89. It's composed of about 800 member clubs throughout the country that promote activities for beginners and run their own races for the more experienced.

Participants in the events must be USCF-licensed riders (this requires a license fee, a completed form, and proof of citizenship and age). Anybody can join. Everyone starts in the entry-level category, then is upgraded appropriately. Riders over the age of 30 are divided into five-year incremental classes and compete against peers. Women do not race against men but form their own age groups.

Members receive a monthly publication that lists the upcoming events. The clubs and local bike shops also can provide information about races.

For information: USCF, 1750 E. Boulder St., Colorado Springs, CO 80909; 303-578-4581.

TENNIS, ANYONE?

An estimated four million of the nation's tennis players are over 50, with the number increasing every year as more of us decide to forego rocking chairs for a few fast sets on the courts. You need only a court, a racquet, a can of balls, and an opponent to play tennis, but, if you'd like to be competitive or sociable, you may want to get into some senior tournaments.

UNITED STATES TENNIS ASSOCIATION

The USTA offers a wide variety of tournaments for players over the advanced age of 35, at both local and national levels. To participate, you must be a member ($20 per year). When you join, you will become an automatic member of a regional section, receive periodic schedules of USTA-sponsored tournaments and events in your area for which you can sign up, get a discount on tennis books and publications, and receive a monthly newsletter and a free subscription to *Tennis* magazine.

In the schedule of tournaments, you'll find competitions listed for specific five-year age groups: for men

from 35 to 80-plus and for women from 35 to 70-plus. There are also self-rated tournaments that match you up with people of all ages who play at your level. If you feel you're good enough to compete, send for an application and sign up. There is usually a modest fee.
For information: USTA, 707 Alexander Rd., Princeton, NJ 08540; 609-452-2580.

RECREATIONAL SENIOR TENNIS LEAGUE

Because so many mature people play tennis (an estimated 700,000 over age 55), the USTA has come up with an inexpensive kit of material showing you how to launch teams of players of the same level of play in parks, tennis clubs, and community centers.
For information: USTA Center for Education and Recreational Tennis, 707 Alexander Rd., Princeton, NJ 08540.

SENIOR NATIONAL CHAMPIONSHIPS

Also sponsored by the USTA are these tournaments for very serious senior players, who are divided into divisions by gender and age. There are four national tournaments per age group—ages 35 to 75 for women and 35 to 85 for men. Singles, doubles, and mixed doubles tournaments are held on four kinds of surfaces—indoor, grass, clay, and hard courts—at facilities throughout the United States. Added attractions: father-son and mother-daughter doubles events.
For information: USTA Seniors Dept., 1212 Ave. of the Americas, New York, NY 10036; 212-302-3322.

SUPER-SENIOR TENNIS

This group, which has been described as an affinity group or a fraternity of male players who compete in the

USTA tournaments, promotes tennis for men from 55 to 85 (or more) and arranges a series of tennis events for them in warm places like Florida during the off-season.

"Our members like to compete and to win," says a spokesperson. "Our constant aim is more tournaments for players in the USTA age divisions for men 55 and over. . . . Super Senior tennis players are the last true amateurs in the sport. No one gets paid to play in a tournament, no one receives travel expenses, and we discourage prize money tournaments."

For information: Super-Senior Tennis, PO Box 5165, Charlottesville, VA 22905.

VAN DER MEER TENNIS UNIVERSITY

Situated on the resort island of Hilton Head, Van der Meer Tennis Center conducts inexpensive five-day Seniors Clinics—as well as weekend clinics—several times a year specifically for players over 50. You'll get many hours of court time plus round robins, social activities, video analyses, tactics and strategies for singles and doubles, individual instruction, and free court time. The idea is to show you how to have more fun on the court. Inexpensive accommodations are available for participants in villas across the street. If you attend a clinic on nonsenior weeks or weekends, you will get a 10 percent discount simply by showing your AARP card.

For information: Van der Meer Tennis University, PO Box 5902, Hilton Head Island, SC 29938-5902; 1-800-845-6138 (in South Carolina, 803-785-9602).

MORE TENNIS VACATIONS

If playing tennis is an essential part of a vacation for you, check out the offerings of the National Senior Sports Association and the Over the Hill Gang (see the beginning of this chapter).

MOTORCYCLE HEAVEN

RETREADS MOTORCYCLE CLUB

Retreads are motorcycle enthusiasts who have reached the ripe old age of 40 and who get together to talk cycling mainly through correspondence. Sometimes, though, they meet at area, regional, and international rallies, with or without their bikes. If you join—there is no membership fee—a club newsletter will keep you informed of the activities going on among the 30,000 members in the U.S., Canada, and a few other countries. **For information:** Retreads Motorcycle Club International, 8749 SW 21st St., Topeka, KS 66615; 913-478-4508.

CANOE VACATIONS

CANOE COUNTRY ESCAPES

If you are a person who likes active vacations and is over 50 (or are accompanying someone who has reached that age), check out the Senior Lodge-to-Lodge and Senior Base Camp packages that take you on wilderness canoe trips in the Boundary Waters between Minnesota and Ontario. On the lodge-to-lodge adventures, you take six days to paddle through the rivers and lakes along the Canadian border, camping out some nights and lodging at rustic inns on others. First and last nights are spent at Gunflint Lodge, a great lake resort noted for its fishing and fantastic food. Once aboard the canoes, an experienced guide leads the way and a packer sets up the campsites and tents and cooks delicious meals over an open fire. Take your fishing rod and your binoculars. **For information:** Canoe Country Escapes, 194 S. Franklin St., Denver, CO 80209; 303-722-6482.

ELDERHOSTEL

Some of the programs offered by Elderhostel include canoeing in their course offerings. Recently, for example, canoeing has been one of the curriculum choices for wilderness trips in Maine and Colorado.

For information: Elderhostel, 75 Federal St., Boston MA 02110; 617-426-8056.

WHAT'S GOING ON FOR GOLFERS

GREENS FEES

Most municipal and many private golf courses give senior golfers (usually those over 65) a discount off the regular greens fees. Take your identification with you and always make inquiries before you play.

THE GOLF CARD

This card, designed especially for senior golfers with lots of time to play on every possible golf course, costs $75 the first year for a single membership or $120 for two and thereafter $70 single and $112 double per year. It entitles you to play two complimentary 18-hole rounds at each of about 1,700 member golf courses throughout the world.

You'll also receive the bimonthly *Golf Traveler* magazine, which contains a directory and guide to the participating courses and resorts.

Added attraction: Discounts at many resorts when you book golf travel packages.

Just to give you an idea of its membership: the average member of this group is 61 and has played golf for 24 years, plays 81 rounds a year, travels 11 weeks a year, travels with a spouse, and plans golf as part of his or her leisure travel.

For information: The Golf Card, 1137 E. 2100 South, PO Box 6439, Salt Lake City, UT 84106; 1-800-453-4260 (in Utah, 801-486-9391).

GOLF HOLIDAYS

The National Senior Sports Association (see pages 151–152) sponsors golf holidays at courses around the U.S. and in Scotland, Ireland, and Mexico. The four-day golf holidays in the U.S. are scheduled once or twice a month at highly rated courses, with the moderate cost covering fees, most meals, four nights' lodging, and cocktail parties. The longer trips to courses overseas are offered three times a year. Golfers are paired by handicaps, with a separate division for those players without established handicaps.

For information: NSSA, 10560 Main St., Suite 205, Fairfax, VA 22030; 703-385-7540.

SWIMMING FOR FUN AND FITNESS

Swimming, a great way to get exercise and stay in shape, is, for most of us, simply a matter of jumping into the nearest lake or pool and butterflying around, maybe doing a few laps. But if you'd like to be organized about it, you'll find that many Ys and other pool operators have special swim classes or meets for adults. Or you can get really serious and join the Masters Swimmers.

U.S. MASTERS SWIMMING

Originally an organization for young competitive swimmers fresh out of college looking for people to race against, today the Masters is a group that is about 80 percent recreational swimmers, many of whom are over 50. Members get swimming insurance and receive a national newsletter and a magazine that offer information about places to swim, groups to swim with, tips on techniques, and the like. There are 54 local associations across the United States for you to hook up with and several weekend or week-long swim camps to consider.

If you're into competition, at whatever age or level of ability, you may participate in local, regional, and even national meets. Competitors are grouped in heats according to their times, regardless of age or sex. But results are tabulated separately for men and women and in five-year age groups right through 90-plus.

For information: USMS National Office, 2 Peter Ave., Rutland, MA 01543; 508-886-6631.

GETTING INTO THE NATIONAL GAMES

U.S. NATIONAL SENIOR SPORTS CLASSIC— THE SENIOR OLYMPICS

The U.S. National Senior Olympics is a not-for-profit organization, sponsored by major corporations, that promotes health and fitness for seniors through competitive multisport events across the country, including the Senior Olympics. Every two years it organizes the National Games for athletes over age 55 who have first qualified in local games.

To qualify for the more than 500 separate events—in track and field, swimming, cycling, golf, tennis, bowling, volleyball, horseshoes, archery, 10-kilometer run, badminton, softball, shuffleboard, and table tennis— athletes 55 and up must compete first at sanctioned state and regional Senior Olympics across the country. The events are organized for men and women in five-year age brackets from 55 to 80-plus.

If you want to be ready to go for the next senior games, get the ground rules from your local Senior Olympics organization or the national group.

For information: U.S. National Senior Olympics, 14323 S. Outer Forty Rd., Suite N300, Chesterfield, MO 63017; 314-878-4900.

STATE SENIOR GAMES

Many states hold their own senior games once a year or so and send their best competitors to national events. If you don't find your state among those listed here, that doesn't mean there's no program in your area—many are sponsored by counties, cities, even local agencies and colleges. Check with your local city, county, or state recreation department to see what's going on near you. You don't have to be a serious competitor to enter the state or local games but merely ready to enjoy yourself. So what if you don't go home with a medal? At the very least, you'll meet other energetic people and have a lot of laughs.

CALIFORNIA
The Southern California Regional Senior Olympics is sponsored by the city of Palm Springs. The first games in 1987 were held over three days and included anyone 55 to 80 (one female swimming contestant was 89) competing in rodeo, ice skating, free-throw shooting, rope skipping, and basketball, as well as all the other sports that could lead to participation in the National Senior Olympics.

For information: Southern California Regional Senior Olympics, Community Services Dept., PO Box 1786, Palm Springs, CA 92263; 619-323-8272.

COLORADO

The Rocky Mountain Senior Games, held in both the summer and the winter, recently celebrated its 10th anniversary. The event is open to residents of Colorado and Wyoming who are 55 and over, with a registration fee of $10. The three-day summer games are held at the University of Northern Colorado in Greeley, Colorado, where you'll pay a minimal fee for lodging, and include such events as track and field, swimming, tennis, basketball, biking, bowling—plus a considerable number of training clinics, workshops, banquets, and dances.

For information: Rocky Mountain Senior Games, 2604 S. Pennsylvania, Denver, CO 80210; 303-777-0471.

The Senior Winter Games at the Summit take place each year during three days in the second week of February at Breckenridge Ski Resort. Anyone from anywhere who's over 55 and wants to compete against his or her peers is welcome. Events include cross-country skiing, downhill slalom, speed skating, snowshoe races, biathlon, figure skating, and more, plus social activities. Age categories for the competitions begin at 55 to 59 and increase in five-year increments to 80 plus. A registration fee that allows participation in as many events as you wish currently stands at $15.

For information: Beth Koran, Summit County Senior Citizens, PO Box 1845, Frisco, CO 80443; 303-668-5486.

CONNECTICUT
The Connecticut Senior Olympics includes not only competitive sport events but also a mini health-fair and physical fitness activities. Connecticut residents and those from neighboring states who are 55-plus converge on the University of Bridgeport on the first Saturday in June for a day of events such as the 5,000-meter run, the 100-yard dash, a mile run, the long jump, diving, bocci, and tennis. There is no entrance fee.

For information: Connecticut Senior Olympics, Harvey Hubbell Gymnasium, University of Bridgeport, Bridgeport, CT 06601.

FLORIDA
The Golden Age Games in Sanford are the biggest and the oldest Senior Games in the country. Held annually in November, they go on for a week and include plenty of competitions, ceremonies, social events, and entertainments. If you are over 55, you are eligible to participate regardless of residency. In other words, you needn't be a Florida resident to compete for the gold, silver, and bronze medals in such sports as basketball, biking, bowling, canoeing, checkers, diving, dance, swimming, tennis, triathlon, track and field, canasta, and croquet. There is a small entry fee for each event.

For information: The Greater Sanford Chamber of Commerce, PO Drawer CC, Sanford, FL 32772-0868; 305-322-2212.

Palm Beach also has big games every fall. Called the U.S. Senior Athletic Games, they are open to everyone who is 50 or over and feature competitions in everything from biking to archery, skydiving, polo, golf, shuffleboard, basketball, billiards, swimming, tennis, running and walking races, table tennis, and track and field events. Registration is $15 for an unlimited number of events. You will compete within your own five-year age range.

For information: U.S. Senior Athletic Games, 200 Castlewood Dr., North Palm Beach, FL 33408; 407-842-3030.

MICHIGAN
Michigan Senior Olympics, a one-day happening open to people over 55, is held in August on the campus of Oakland Community College in Farmington Hills. For small registration and event fees you get lunch and a chance to compete for a medal in athletic events such as discus throwing, 100-yard dash, diving, and cycling. You can also take home ribbons for your superior cookies, cakes, or breads or your prowess at checkers, arts and crafts, and dancing.

For information: Michigan Senior Olympics, O.P.C., 312 Woodward, Rochester, MI 48063; 313-656-1403.

MISSOURI
The St. Louis Senior Olympics has become an institution in Missouri by now. A four-day event that is open to anyone who lives anywhere and is 55 years old, it costs a nominal amount and is action-oriented. No knitting contests here—only energetic events such as bicycle races, 200-meter races, standing long jumps, tennis singles and doubles, and swimming.

For information: Senior Olympics, JCAA, 2 Millstone Campus, St. Louis, MO 63146.

MONTANA
The Big Sky State Games are held each July in Billings, again for people over 55.
For information: The Big Sky Games, PO Box 2318, Billings, MT 59101.

NEW YORK
New York Senior Games for state residents over the age of 55 are usually held on a state college campus over a weekend in the spring. Competition is divided into age categories starting with 55 to 59 and going up to 80-plus with activities ranging from archery and badminton to cycling, billiards, and volleyball. Also included are a dinner with entertainment and dancing, workshops, and clinics—all for a modest fee.
For information: New York Senior Games, State Parks, Agency 1, 12th Fl., Albany, NY 12238; 518-474-2324.

NORTH CAROLINA
After local games held all over the state, the winners of the North Carolina Senior Games travel to Raleigh for the state finals and/or to the national games. Every sport from billiards to spin casting to track is on the agenda.
For information: North Carolina Senior Games, PO Box 33590, Raleigh, NC 27606; 919-851-5456.

PENNSYLVANIA
The Pennsylvania Senior Games "combines sports, recreation, and entertainment with fellowship." You can get some of each if you are a Pennsylvania resident who is 55

or older. The games are held over four days at a university campus where you can get lodging and three meals a day for remarkably low cost. If you prefer to stay in a motel, you'll get a senior discount.

For information: Pennsylvania Senior Games, 231 State St., Harrisburg, PA 17101-1195.

VERMONT

The Green Mountain Senior Games in Poultney, whose major sponsor is Killington Ski Area, require you to be a Vermont resident who is over 55 and an amateur at your sport. For a small $5 registration fee, you play, eat lunch, and have fun. Competitive events—organized in age groups of 55 to 62, 63 to 70, and 71 and over—include everything from golf and tennis to swimming, darts, horseshoes, walking, running, table tennis, bowling, croquet, softball and shuffleboard. Just for fun, there are folk and square dancing, volleyball, walking, free swims. The games are held in the early fall.

For information: Green Mountain Senior Games, PO Box 1660, Station A, Rutland, VT 05701.

VIRGINIA

Virginia Golden Olympics is a four-day happening in the spring, this one at Lynchburg College, where athletes compete to qualify for the U.S. National Senior Olympics—or just for the fun of it. The event combines social events and entertainment with sports events. The fees are low, lodging and meals are cheap, and the sporting events are many. Some of the more novel competitions include jump rope, miniature golf, riflery, and Frisbee throws along with the usual swimming, tennis, running, and the like, for various age groups from 55 to 85-plus.

For information: Golden Olympics, PO Box 2774, Lynchburg, VA 24501; 804-847-1640.

WASHINGTON
A truly athletic happening, the Seattle Senior Sports Festival is a Regional Qualifying Event for the national games and involves only serious sports including track and field, tennis, lawn bowling, pickleball, swimming, table tennis, and softball. The small entry fee covers as many sports as you'd like to enter. You are eligible if you are 55 or over and are an amateur in your chosen sport. **For information:** Senior Sports Festival, 100 Dexter Ave. North, Seattle, WA 98109-5199; 206-625-2981.

EVENTS FOR RAPID RUNNERS
MASTERS TRACK & FIELD AND ROAD RACES
Masters are men and women 30 and over who participate in organized track and field meets and road races. There are no qualifications to join. "About all you need is a pair of shorts, a pair of shoes, and an occasional entry fee if you decide to compete in a meet or race," says *National Masters News*, a monthly newspaper and the main source of information about events, providing results, schedules, and local information for each region of the country. "Masters competition is divided into 5- or 10-year age groups for men and women. Every event from the 100-yard dash to the shot put to the marathon is available."

If you want to compete after working out on your own or in a club, there are many meets and races with prizes awarded by age categories. For most of them, you simply show up at the right time and place, register, and participate, although you may wish to sign up in advance.

When you're really experienced, you travel to regional, national, and international competitions, where you'll pay your own expenses and compete as an individual. "The championship events are open to everyone," says long-distance running committee chairman Bob Boal.

For information: Masters Long Distance Running, TAC/USA, 4261 S. 184th St., Seattle, WA 98188. To subscribe to the monthly newspaper, write to *National Masters News*, PO Box 5185, Pasadena, CA 91107.

FIFTY-PLUS RUNNERS ASSOCIATION
This is not a club, although it occasionally sponsors over-50 runs. It is an organization that was formed by high-level exercise researchers at Stanford University "to provide a basis for exchanging information about running and its benefits (and hazards) among the obviously large and growing number of over-50 runners. Another objective was to establish a cadre of people who could serve as a basis for studies of the impact of running on many aspects of life."

Its members, who live in almost every state and in several foreign countries, receive a quarterly newsletter and are asked to participate in ongoing surveys and studies. Members are asked to contribute $20 a year (tax-deductible) to defray costs.

For information: Fifty-Plus Runners Association, PO Box D, Stanford, CA 94305.

OVER-50 SOFTBALL

SENIOR SOFTBALL-USA

Senior Softball-USA is the largest senior softball organization in the world. It conducts softball tournaments all over the country, organizes international tournaments, and co-sponsors the Seniors Softball World Series each year. Anyone over 50, man or woman, in the U.S. and Canada is welcome to join for $8 a year or $20 for three years. Members get assistance in finding teams (there are about 6,000 in the U.S.) in their areas and receive the *Senior Softball* newspaper, which keeps them up to date on tournaments and other news. They are eligible to take part in an annual international tour that takes teams and spouses to play ball and tour faraway places such as New Zealand, France, and Italy.

For information: Senior Softball-USA, 9 Fleet St., Sacramento, CA 95831; 916-393-8566.

NATIONAL ASSOCIATION OF SENIOR CITIZEN SOFTBALL

To play ball in one of the teams sponsored by this organization, you must be at least 50, and there's no upper age limit. The NASCS is an association of several thousand teams around the country, with a goal of promoting a worldwide interest in senior softball. It hosts a national tournament every July and puts on yearly exhibition games and tournaments in several foreign countries. A quarterly newsletter keeps members up to date on happenings.

For information: NASCS, PO Box 1085, Mt. Clemens, MI 48046; 313-792-2110 or 313-286-8757.

Chapter Fourteen
Adventures on Skis

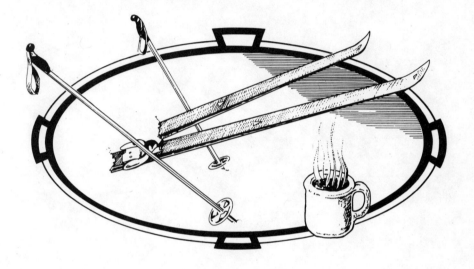

OVER THE TOP ON
TWO NARROW BOARDS

Downhill skiing is one sport you'd think would appeal only to less mature, less wise, less breakable people. On the contrary, there is an astounding number of ardent over-50 skiers who would much rather glide down mountains than sit around waiting for springtime. In fact, many of us ski more than ever now that we're older because we can go midweek when the crowds are thinner and we get impressive discounts on lift tickets. And many of us are taking up the sport for the first time. Ski schools all over the United States and Canada are reporting an increase of older students in beginner classes.

The truth is, skiing is one sport you're never too old to learn or to practice. Once you get the hang of it, you can ski at your own speed, choosing the terrain, the difficulty level, and the challenge. You can swoop down cliffs through narrow icy passes or wend your way down gentle slopes in a more leisurely fashion, aided by the new improved skis and boots, clearly marked and carefully groomed trails, and those newfangled lifts that take all the work out of getting up the mountain.

Besides, ski resorts are falling all over themselves to lure older skiers to their slopes, offering discounts, free passes, and other engaging incentives. Many over-50 groups sponsor ski activities as well.

CLUBS FOR MATURE SKIERS

THE OVER THE HILL GANG

As we have noted, this group originated with a group of older skiers who wanted companionship on the slopes, and skiing is still its main emphasis. In fact, its motto is "Once you're over the hill, you pick up speed!"

If you've hit 50, you are eligible to join (your spouse may be younger) and set forth on ski adventures—both downhill and cross-country—in this country and abroad. Members get discounts on lifts and rentals and sometimes are the recipients of free group guides and special lift-line privileges. People who have never put on a pair of ski boots or haven't tried them in years can take advantage of refresher clinics or group lessons arranged by the club.

And when the ski season ends, you can join the Gang for a bike trip, a party, maybe rafting or ballooning or a sailing trip in the Caribbean. This club, with an age range of 50 to 94 and an average age of 63, is definitely out for fun.

Every year the club organizes several Senior Ski Weeks in the Rockies, Europe, Canada, and New Zealand. Future plans include the South American ski resorts. The event packages include transportation, accommodations, discounted (or free) lift tickets, parties, food, and, in some cases, ski escorts and lessons.

The local Gangs also run their own ski trips both in their own vicinities and elsewhere in the world, and all members everywhere are invited to go along. Often there are certain days of the week that the Gangs gather, meeting at a ski area's base lodge and dividing into groups with their own member guides. They rally at reserved spots for lunch, ski some more, then get together for après-ski gatherings and a bit of bragging.

Membership in the national organization costs $37 ($60 for couple) plus chapter dues if a chapter is located in your area. A quarterly news magazine is part of the deal.

For information: Over the Hill Gang International, 6635 S. Dayton St., Ste. 220, Englewood, CO 80111; 303-790-2724.

70+ SKI CLUB

You have to prove you are 70 before you're invited to join this club, which now has about 4,500 members in their 70s and 80s and a few in their 90s, all of them active downhill skiers. The club meets at various ski areas—usually in New York or New England—for races, companionship, and partying and organizes big trips in the United States and Europe.

Lloyd T. Lambert, a former ski writer who was born in 1901, founded the 70+ Ski Club in 1977 with 34 members. One purpose was to make skiing less expensive for older people on limited retirement incomes. He urged ski areas to let members ski free or at discounts, and his campaign worked. Today most ski areas give us offers we can't refuse. Says Lambert, "We provide inspiration to the 40-year-olds who are about to give up the sport because they think they're getting feeble."

Hunter Mountain in New York's Catskills hosts the club's annual one-day meeting early in March every year. This is when the yearly 70+ Ski Races are held, an event so popular that the contestants are divided into three categories—men 70 to 80, women 70 to 80, and everyone over 80. There are serious slalom races as well as "fun" races with awards for the winners presented at a gala party at the lodge.

Most gatherings of the members take place at ski areas in New England and feature special races and special events, but there are always a couple of week-long ventures to the Alps and the Rockies. And the club has members all over the United States and Canada, even some in Europe.

Club members pay only $5—for life. Proof of your date of birth is required with your application, and you must not apply more than two weeks before your 70th birthday! You'll receive a 70+ Ski Club patch, a membership card, a newsletter, and a list of ski areas throughout the country where you can ski free or at a discount. You can also get a list of members for an additional fee so you can arrange your own companionship if you wish.

For information: Lloyd T. Lambert, 70+ Ski Club, 104 Eastside Dr., Ballston Lake, NY 12019; 518-399-5458.

BROMLEY SENIOR SKIERS CLUB
Free membership in this Bromley Mountain, Vermont, club provides skiers over 65 with half-price lift tickets or a half-price season pass good after January 1, discounts on lift-lesson-equipment packages for family members, and preferred parking. Report to Customer Service with your ID for a club card and a parking permit.
For information: Bromley Mountain, Box 1130, Manchester Center, VT 05255; 802-824-5522.

SILVER PEAKS
Any intrepid skier who is over the age of 55 is invited to join the Silver Peaks, a group that skis together every

Tuesday at Jay Peak, in Vermont, for fun and instruction. Membership is free. From ages 55 to 65, your lift tickets cost you much less than the regular rate. Skiers 65 and older can ski for only $5 anytime. After complimentary coffee and donuts in the morning, you ski in compatible groups guided by instructors, stopping for lunch and an après-ski gathering.
For information: Call Jay Peak: 802-988-2611.

MOUNT SNOW SENIORSKI
Mount Snow offers a couple of special weeks during December and March to skiers over 50. You'll get a discounted five-day lift ticket (it costs $110 at this writing) and many other activities. There's a Monday afternoon guided ski tour, a wine-tasting party, an ice cream social, evening sleigh ride, and races. You also get free overnight ski storage and a card good for discounts in shops in the ski area. You'll have your own lounge area in the Base Lodge to meet each morning for complimentary coffee and donuts.
For information: Mount Snow, VT 05356; 1-800-444-9404 (in NY, NJ, Canada, and New England states: 802-464-8501).

"IT'S NEVER TOO LATE," PARK CITY
This program is designed to teach older beginners to ski, with specially tailored instructions for those who thought they were too old to learn to glide down mountains gracefully. The two-hour group lessons at Utah's Park City Ski Area are available for over-50s Monday through Friday from noon to 2 P.M. or in private lessons anytime.
For information: "It's Never Too Late," Park City Ski Area, Box 39, Park City, UT 84060; 801-649-8111

SENIOR SKIER DEVELOPMENT PROGRAM, SKI WINDHAM

In this program for senior skiers at Windham Mountain, in New York, you ski in groups with a leader-instructor every Tuesday for seven weeks in January and February. You get continental breakfast and lunch in the package as well as lift tickets and individual events such as videos, lectures, individual instructions, and a party. The program is run by the Windham Ski School and the Eastern Professional Ski Instructors Association.

For information: PSIA-Eastern Division, 1-A Lincoln Ave., Albany NY 12205-4900; 518-452-6095.

STRATTON SENIOR SKIERS ASSOCIATION

When you join this group at Stratton Mountain, Vermont, for an annual fee of $35, you'll get cheaper lift tickets (those over 70 pay only $5 per day) and a 10 percent discount on food in the base lodges. You meet with other members and ski together, take part in special senior clinics, and attend parties. Every spring, the association organizes a Senior Day that includes races and a reception.

Stratton also has its Club 62, which offers group skiing to skiers over the age of 62, with instructor tours and ski school lessons, on Monday, Wednesday, and Friday mornings and afternoons.

For information: Stratton Senior Skiers, Stratton Mountain, VT 05155; 802-297-2200.

WATERVILLE VALLEY SILVER STREAKS

The Silver Streaks of Waterville Valley, New Hampshire, are members of a no-fee club for skiers who have reached their 55th birthday (and spouses at any age).

Silver Streakers may buy a midweek lift ticket for $4 off regular midweek price the first time they ski. On subsequent nonholiday midweek visits, the lift ticket is reduced at least $2 each time until it reaches $14, the price paid the rest of the season. Mondays through Thursdays, you get even more: reserved parking, free coffee and donuts, social events, race clinics, warm-up runs with the staff, and Silver Streak NASTAR races. Membership also entitles you to reduced prices on rentals and class lessons and a one-third reduction on lodging, also midweek.

For beginners over 55, the resort offers a learn-to-ski package with lifts, ski lesson, and rental equipment, all for $26 a day at this writing.

Members of the 70+ Ski Club—and any other intrepid skiers over 70—ski free midweek except on holidays.
For information: Waterville Valley Silver Streaks, Waterville Valley, NH 03215; off-season, 603-236-8311; winter, 603-236-8330. For lodging reservations, call 1-800-468-2553 or 603-236-8371.

THE WILD OLD BUNCH
This merry band of senior skiers who navigate the steep slopes of Alta in Utah is an informal bunch of men and women from Utah and many other states who ski together for fun, welcoming anybody who wants to join them. There are no rules, no designated leaders, no lessons, no regular meetings, and no age restrictions, though most members are well past 50, retired business or professional people. Somewhere between 50 and 100 avid skiers now wear the Wild Old Bunch patch.

The group grows haphazardly as members pick up any stray skiers they find on the slopes, showing them their mountain and passing along their enthusiasm for the steeper trails and the off-trail skiing in Alta's famous powder. Says a spokesperson, Rush Spedden, "If you visit Alta and would like to join in some of the old-fashioned camaraderie of skiing, just look for any of us on the slopes or on the deck of the mid-mountain Alpenglow Inn, where we gather for lunch and tales. Either ski with us or grab a seat for some lively conversation."

Although the bunch isn't sexist, some of the wives prefer to stay on less difficult slopes or to travel the cross-country trails, so they wear "Wild Wives" patches. **For information:** Look for the Wild Old Bunch on the slopes, or, if absolutely necessary, contact Rush Spedden, 4131 Cumorah Dr., Salt Lake City, UT 84124; 801-278-2283.

OKEMO MOUNTAIN
If you are 65 or older, you may join Okemo's Masters Program for $25 a year. Membership includes half-price skiing for skiers 65 to 69 and free skiing (except on certain peak days when you'll pay half-price) to skiers 70 and over. You also get half-price on all group ski lessons and NASTAR on Thursdays, and a one-time free use of demo skis.
For information: Okemo Mountain, RFD 1, Ludlow, VT 05149; 802-228-4041.

MORE DISCOUNTS AND FREEBIES FOR DOWNHILL SKIERS

There's hardly a ski area in the country today that doesn't give mature folks a good deal. Many cut the price of lift tickets in half at age 60, others at 62 or 65, and some stop charging at all when you are 65 or 70.

To give you an idea of what some of the ski areas offer you, here is a short list of possibilities throughout North America. This does not include all areas, of course, so be sure to check out others in locations that interest you. *Always ask* if there is a senior discount before buying your lift ticket.

Proof of age will be required in most cases, so remember to take along some identification that includes your date of birth.

CALIFORNIA

Among the ski areas in California that give senior skiers good deals on lift tickets are Mammoth Mountain, where there is no charge over 65; Alpine Meadows, half price over 65, no charge at 70; Badger Pass, no charge over 60; Iron Mountain, with discounted lift tickets at 65, special lessons and packages; Dodge Ridge, discounts at 62; Sierra Summit, discount starts at 55; and Tahoe Donner, with discounts at 60 plus.

COLORADO

The ski areas offering discounted senior lift tickets, some starting at 60 and usually charging nothing at 70, include Arapahoe Basin, Arrowhead, Aspen Highlands, Aspen Mountain, Beaver Creek, Berthoud Pass, Breckenridge, Buttermilk, Ski Cooper, Copper Mountain, Crested Butte, Eldora Mountain, Keystone, Loveland, Monarch, Powderhorn, Purgatory, Silver Creek, Ski Sunlight, Snowmass, Steamboat, Telluride, Vail, Winter Park, and Wolf Creek. In fact, as you can see, it's a rare ski area that has no senior discounts.

In addition, a few areas have instituted special senior

ski weeks. For example, Steamboat's Seniors Plus Vacation Week for over-45s is a good deal that includes five days of lessons, lifts, races, meals, and parties. Purgatory now has its SnoMasters Ski Weeks for skiers over 55—choose that package and you get discounts on everything from lift tickets to lodging.

IDAHO
Skiers 65 and over get good discounts at the famous ski resort at Sun Valley.

MAINE
Sunday River Ski Resort in Bethel has a White Caps program for skiers 65 and over that gives you an all-day lift ticket, three hours of instruction, and lunch for a low price. Other areas with reduced lift tickets for older skiers include Shawnee Peak, Sugarloaf, and Saddleback.

MICHIGAN
At Crystal Mountain in Thompsonville, senior skiers— 55 and older—get a 50 percent discount on all-day lift tickets, lessons, and rentals, valid anytime. Other good deals may be found at Mt. Zion, Timber Ridge, and Shanty Creek.

More than 30 ski areas all over Michigan now offer a February week of free lift tickets and/or lessons for skiers over 60.

NEVADA
Lift tickets at Mt. Rose are reduced if you're over 62. At Ski Incline, every Wednesday is Senior Social Day for

over-55s, when for a small fee, you get skiing, morning coffee, brunch, and speakers. Also try Lee Canyon and Diamond Peak.

NEW HAMPSHIRE

Look for a good deal on lift tickets at Loon Mountain, where skiers over 65 pay about half for season passes and those over 70 don't pay a cent. Waterville Valley cuts the rate back at only 55 and allows free skiing at 70 midweek. Check out the Waterville Silver Streaks too (pages 184–185). Other good deals may be found at Mt. Cranmore, Bretton Woods, and Dartmouth.

NEW YORK

At Gore Mountain, you'll get the junior rate if you're over 62 and ski free if you're over 70. The same good deal is available at Ski Windham but starting at 65. Other areas that discount the lift tickets include Catamount, Hunter, and Belleayre.

PENNSYLVANIA

Discounted lift tickets are yours at Camelback, Blue Marsh, and Hidden Valley, among others, in this state. Eagle Rock cuts the price at age 50.

UTAH

Park City and Snow Basin offer half-price lift tickets to people who have made it past 65. The lifts are reduced at 62 at Snowbird and are free at Park City over 70. Other ski areas that encourage senior skiing with discounts include Sundance, Jackson Hole, and Solitude.

VERMONT

Vermont's ski areas are old hands at discounts for mature skiers. Among them:

Stratton Mountain gives you half-price lift tickets if you are 62 to 69 and an even bigger discount when you're 70. And there are additional advantages if you join the Stratton Senior Skiers Association (see page 184).

At Bolton Valley, skiers 70 and over receive a 50 percent discount on all lift tickets. Bolton also runs a January Senior Week that's inexpensive and fun.

Okemo Mountain: 65 to 69 ski at half price, while over-70s ski free. See page 186 for the Okemo Ski Masters program.

Pico: Anyone 65 to 69 is charged half price for lift tickets, ski lessons, and equipment rentals. Members of the 70+ Ski Club ski free on weekdays and for half price on weekends.

Killington: Skiers over 65 pay the junior prices (about 50 percent off) for lift tickets, lessons, packages, and rentals.

Haystack: If you're over 65, you ski free during the week. There's a nominal charge on weekends and holidays.

Mount Snow: Discounted lift tickets for seniors, plus a couple of SeniorSki Weeks scheduled for December and March (see page 183).

Bromley: See page 167 for the Bromley Senior Skiers Club.

Jay Peak offers $5 lift tickets for skiers 65 and over and also sponsors races for the older crowd. Check out the Silver Peaks Club, pages 182–183.

Mad River Glen give seniors over 64 a discounted rate on both day and season passes.

Mt. Mansfield at Stowe discounts lift tickets except during holiday periods if you're 65 to 69 and charges nothing for those over 70.

At Ascutney, skiers 62 and older are offered lift tickets for $10 a day. If you're over 70, it's free.

Burke Mountain is always free if you're over 65.

At Maple Valley, skiers 60 to 69 ski at half price every day while those over 70 ski free.

Middlebury Snow Bowl sells a discounted season pass to skiers over 62 and gives free passes to over-70s.

Sugarbush: Here you get a reduced rate from age 65 to 69 and pay nothing at all over 70.

Smuggler's Notch: At 55, you are entitled to $1 off the price of the season pass for every year you have lived. At 65, you may buy lift tickets at half price. At 70, Vermont residents stop paying altogether. Valid every day.

VIRGINIA
At Massanutten Mountain in Harrisonburg, those 65 and over pay about two-thirds of the regular rates for lift tickets and ski rentals.

WASHINGTON
In Washington state, many ski areas give senior discounts. Among them are Crystal Mountain, Mission Ridge, and White Pass.

WISCONSIN
Here, the discounts are to be found at Mt. Ashwabay, Crystal Ridge, Cascade Mountain, Wintergreen, Trollhaugen, and Tyrol Basin, among others. Some even start cutting the prices at age 50.

WYOMING
The Jackson Hole Ski Area and Grand Targhee have good deals for over-65s. Probably all of the other areas have now jumped on the bandwagon, so check them out before you make your plans.

OTHER ALPINE ADVENTURES

ELDERHOSTEL DOWNHILL SKIING
The Sunday River Inn in Newry, Maine, was the first Elderhostel campus to offer alpine skiing. The week-long programs available several times during the winter include daily skiing and instruction at Sunday River Ski Resort, plus your choice of courses. These programs, like all the other Elderhostel residence courses, are great bargains. Downhill skiing programs are offered at other ski areas as well.
For information: Elderhostel, 75 Federal St., 3rd Floor, Boston, MA 02110; 617-426-8056.

DOWNHILL RACES FOR ALL AGES (YOURS INCLUDED)

NASTAR
NASTAR (National Standard Race) is a ski-racing program sponsored by *Ski* magazine for recreational downhill skiers whatever their age, with 5,000 races held in ski areas all over the United States for medals based on

age, sex, and handicap. The age divisions that apply to *you* are the following: men and women 50 to 59, women 60 and over, men 60 to 69, and men 70 and over. You may race on your own or as part of a participating ski club.

If you want to join in the fun, ask for the NASTAR Registration Desk at your ski area, fill out the registration card that registers you for the season, pay a fee, and get a souvenir race bib. Each time you race, your day's best handicap will automatically be recorded at the NASTAR Computer Center, where your best three handicaps of the season will be averaged. If you are a winner in your age group (finalists include 10 men and 10 women from each age category), you will be treated to an expense-paid trip to the finals.

For information: NASTAR, PO Box 4580, Aspen, CO 81612; 303-925-7864.

UNITED STATES SKI ASSOCIATION ALPINE MASTERS

If you're a good competitive skier, how about signing up to race in the masters races for older skiers sponsored in various parts of the country every winter by divisions of the U.S. Ski Association? You'll be competing against people your own age. In addition to the races held in the United States, the International Masters Cup series has entrants from the U.S. and many European countries. To be eligible for masters races, skiers must join the U.S. Ski Association and get a racing license.

For information: United States Ski Association, PO Box 100, 1500 Kearns Blvd., Park City, UT 84060.

CROSS-COUNTRY SKI ADVENTURES

Many cross-country areas also give senior skiers a break. Always ask about discounts before paying admission, because you may save a few of your hard-earned dollars.

CROSS-COUNTRY VACATIONS FOR WOMEN ONLY

If you're female and 40, you qualify for the ski trips run by Outdoor Vacations for Women over 40, and that should make you very happy. This company offers some pretty exciting adventures and promises you the fellowship of women your own age.

For women who live in the vicinity of Boston, there are one-day cross-country ski clinics designed for beginners and intermediates. A day includes lessons, lunch, and ski touring, all for very little cost. Then there are ski weekends in New Hampshire where you stay at a cozy inn, take lessons, and ski as far as you want; and recently there have been one-week trips to Glacier National Park and the Boundary Waters Wilderness Area, in Minnesota.

For information: Outdoor Vacations for Women Over 40, PO Box 200, Groton, MA 01450; 508-448-3331.

ELDERHOSTEL

Elderhostel, known for its low-cost learning vacations for people over 60 (and companions who may be younger) at educational institutions (see Chapter 16), has combined cross-country skiing and winter nature explora-

tion since 1978. Since the programs change from year to year, you must check out the offerings in its catalog.
For information: Elderhostel, 75 Federal St., 3rd Floor, Boston, MA 02110; 617-426-8056.

WATERVILLE VALLEY
Cross-country skiers may join Waterville Valley Silver Streaks Club (see pages 184–185) if they are over 55, applying the membership benefits to the resort's 100-kilometer cross-country center.
For information: Waterville Valley, NH 03215; off-season, 603-236-8311; winter, 603-236-8330.

RACES FOR CROSS-COUNTRY SKIERS

To ski in the international races run every year by the World Masters Cross-Country Ski Association, you must be over 30. The competitions are separated into five-year age classes all the way up to 75+, separated also by gender. Participants from all nations are invited, and each country is allowed one scoring A team per class and any number of nonscoring B teams. The championship races are held once a year, in Austria in 1988, Canada in 1989, and Sweden in 1990.

For information: World Masters Cross-Country Ski Association USA, 332 Iowa Ave., PO Box 718, Hayward, WI 54843; 715-634-4891.

Chapter Fifteen

Back to Summer Camp

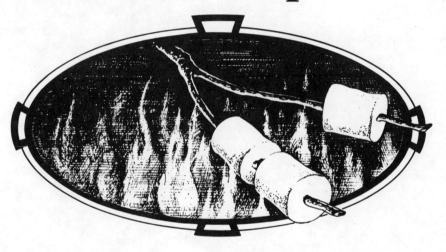

Maybe you thought camp was just for kids, but if you are a grown-up person who likes the outdoors, swimming, boating, birds, and arts and crafts and who appreciates fields and forests and star-filled skies, you too can pack your bags and go off on a sleepaway. Throughout the country, many camps set aside weeks for adult sessions, while others offer adult programs all season long. More and more adults are getting hooked on summer camp, and many wouldn't miss a year.

ELDERHOSTEL

Many of Elderhostel's programs are a combination of camping and college. In this wildly successful low-cost educational program (see Chapter 16 for details), you can spend a week or two camping in remote scenic areas, enjoying all the activities from horseback riding to crafts, boating, campfires, and sleeping under the stars (or in a cabin). As an example, there are Elderhostel weeks at Classroom of the Earth, affiliated with Colvig Silver Camps, in Red Creek Valley near Durango, Colorado. Most Elderhostel weeks are held, however, on college or university campuses in this country and abroad, where you live in a dorm, eat in the college dining rooms, and take courses in subjects that appeal to you.

For information: Elderhostel, 75 Federal St., 3rd Floor, Boston, MA 02110; 617-426-8056.

RV ELDERHOSTELS

Less expensive than regular Elderhostel programs because you take along your own housing, these programs come in two varieties. One is the usual Elderhostel educational vacation on a college campus, where you partake of the happenings, including courses, meals, and excursions, with the rest of the group but sleep in your own RV, trailer, or tent on the campus or at nearby campgrounds. The other is a mobile program or moving field trip—in Alaska, for example, or Wyoming or along the Oregon Trail—where you'll hear the lectures over your CB radio as you travel. Moving along like a wagon train, you travel in a group led by an experienced guide and make many stops for lectures and sight-seeing as you go.

For information: Elderhostel, 75 Federal St., 3rd Floor, Boston, MA 02110; 617-426-8056.

INTERHOSTEL

Sponsored by the University of New Hampshire, Interhostel offers similar arrangements to those of Elderhostel, also inexpensive, but always in foreign countries and for at least two weeks at a stretch (see pages 210–211 in Chapter 16).

For information: Interhostel, University of New Hampshire, 6 Garrison Ave., Durham, NH 03824; 603-862-1147.

GRANDPARENTS CAMP

Every August, you can take your grandchild/grandchildren to camp with you for a week. Designed to help long-distance grandparents get to know their grandchildren and to allow two generations to spend time together free from the restraints of the kids' parents and the responsibilities of everyday life, the camp is sponsored by the Foundation for Grandparenting. The place is Sagamore Institute, a rustic, rambling, nonprofit conference and outdoor recreation center in Raquette Lake, New York, in the Adirondack Mountains. This place was, in a former life, a Vanderbilt family "great camp."

Mornings, children and grandparents engage in joint activities such as walks, hikes, berry-picking, group games, and nature art. Afternoons, each age group is on its own, free to choose from a variety of recreational activities. Before dinner, grandparents get together for discussions on grandparenting issues, and evening sessions again feature togetherness and include such activities as square dancing, stories, campfires, and singalongs.

For information: Sagamore Lodge and Conference Center, Sagamore Rd., Raquette Lake, NY 13436; 315-354-5311; or Foundation for Grandparenting, PO Box 97, Jay, NY 12941; 518-946-2177.

THE SALVATION ARMY

The Salvation Army operates 55 rural camps across the country, most of which have year-round adult sessions. The camps are run by regional divisional headquarters of the Army; thus, each is totally different from the others. Open to anyone, they cost very little.

For information: Contact a local unit of the Salvation Army or write to the national headquarters at 799 Bloomfield Ave., Verona, NJ 07044.

VACATIONS AND
SENIOR CENTERS ASSOCIATION

VASCA is a nonprofit organization that will give you information about camps for people over 55 in the New York area. It represents 17 vacation lodges scattered about New York, New Jersey, Connecticut, and Pennsylvania, most of them for people with an income below a specified level. Some are small rustic wilderness camps, and some are huge sprawling complexes with endless activities. They are sponsored by various nonprofit organizations and foundations, many with religious affiliations, and most are extremely cheap.

For information: VASCA, 275 Seventh Ave., New York, NY 10001; 212-645-6590.

YMCA/YWCA

The Y runs lots of camps, most of them for children, but with special sessions for adults over 50. For example, Westwind on the Pacific is a 500-acre camp owned by the Portland, Oregon, YWCA and located on the coast at the mouth of the Salmon River Estuary. Its senior week, for people over 55, is held every August and costs about $100 for everything. Camp Cheerio, run by the High Point, North Carolina, YMCA, is in the Appalachian Mountains and sets aside three weeks a year for campers over 50, who live in the same cabins and pursue all the same activities as the kids do during the rest of the summer.

For information: Ask your local Y for information about camps in your area.

CAMPS SPONSORED BY CHURCH GROUPS
There are many camps and summer workshops run by church organizations, too many and too diverse to list here. One source of information is Christian Camping International.
For information: Christian Camping International, PO Box 646, Wheaton, IL 60189; 708-462-0300.

AUDUBON ECOLOGY CAMPS AND WORKSHOPS
Not for over-50s alone, these programs are included here because mature nature freaks will love these natural history programs for adults run by the National Audubon Society. Audubon Ecology Camps are located in Connecticut, Maine, and Wyoming, with sessions from 6 to 12 days. The special workshops include nature photography trips in Yellowstone and Grand Teton national parks and other travel adventures in the Olympic Peninsula, Big Bend National Park in Texas, southern Florida, Arizona, and Costa Rica.
For information: National Audubon Society, 613 Riversville Rd., Greenwich, CT 06831; 203-869-2017.

Chapter Sixteen

Going Back to School After 50

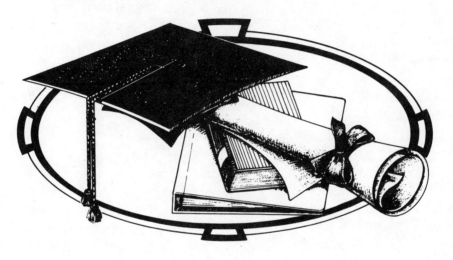

Have you always wanted to learn French, study African birds, examine Eskimo culture, delve into archaeology, international finance, horticulture, the language of whales, or great literature of the 19th century? Now is the time to do it. If you're a typical member of the over-50s generation, you're in good shape, healthy and alert, with the energy and the time to pursue new interests. So why not go back to school and learn all those things you've always wished you knew?

You are welcome as a regular student at just about any institution in the United States and Canada, especially in the continuing-education programs, but many colleges and universities have set up special deals and programs designed to lure older people back to the classroom. Some offer good reductions in tuition (so good indeed that sometimes you may attend classes half price or even free) and give credits for life experience. Others have set up programs designed specifically for mature scholars. In some cases, there are whole schools set up just for you.

Going back to class is an excellent way to generate feelings of accomplishment and to exercise the mind— and one of the best ways to make new friends. It doesn't necessarily mean you'll have to turn in term papers or take excruciatingly difficult exams. Sign up for one class a week on flower arranging or Spanish conversation or a once-a-month lecture series on managing your money. Or register as a part-time or full-time student in a traditional university program. Or take a learning vacation on a college campus. Do it *your* way.

You don't even have to attend classes to learn on vacation. You can go on archeological digs, count butterflies, help save turtles from extinction, brush up on your bassoon playing, listen to opera, search for Roman remains in Europe, study dancing or French cuisine, go on safari in Africa.

THE INSTITUTE OF LIFETIME LEARNING

Part of the many services of the American Association of Retired Persons (see Chapter 19), the Institute of Lifetime Learning acts as a clearinghouse and research center on education for older learners and can be a great help in finding out about educational opportunities. Among its most useful offerings is a booklet, *Tuition Policies in Higher Education for Older Adults*, which tells which traditional colleges and universities throughout the country do or do not offer you free or reduced tuition.

Another booklet, *College Centers for Older Learners*, is a state-by-state listing of learning programs designed specifically for mature students. These range from continuing education to peer-teaching programs.

For information: Institute of Lifetime Learning, 1909 K St. NW, Washington, DC 20049; 202-662-4895.

CAMPUS STUDY/ TRAVEL PROGRAMS

ELDERHOSTEL

Elderhostel, an educational travel program for older people who want to expand their horizons and learn a few more things, offers some of the world's best bargains. It is a network of over 1,200 colleges, universities, museums, hostels, education centers, and other cultural institutions that offer low-cost, short-term, residential academic programs for people 60 and older (and companions over 50). The programs are offered in the United States and Canada as well as 40 countries overseas. Those in the U.S. and Canada are usually for one week, while those in other countries are for two or three weeks.

In most cases, you live on a campus, in a dormitory, and take up to three courses chosen from a selection in the liberal arts and sciences taught by the host institution's faculty. There are no exams, grades, or homework. Nor do you get college credits for them. The courses and places to choose from are amazingly varied and many, an array of impressive proportions. The choices change every season and are rarely the same from year to year. Accommodations range from typical dorms to rustic cabins in the mountains to urban highrises at city universities. You will dine on campus food, simple but nourishing, and may use any of the school's recreational and cultural resources. Getting to and from the campus for the domestic programs is your responsibility.

Some of the domestic programs are action-oriented, offering courses in cross-country or downhill skiing, hiking, biking, or canoeing, for example, and a few involve camping. If you are really into participation, you may even want to consider Elderhostel's Outward Bound program.

The international Elderhostel programs, two or three weeks long, usually combine morning classes with afternoon excursions, with the campus serving as home base as you study the culture, history, and lore of the land instructed by members of the university's faculty. Included in the overseas programs have been such far-out adventures as bike tours through England, France and Holland (see page 157) and trekking trips in Nepal.

There is sure to be a program in a place you've always wanted to visit, giving courses you've always wanted to take, at any time of the year. Check out the Elderhostel catalog.

For information: Elderhostel, 75 Federal St., 3rd Floor, Boston, MA 02110; 617-426-8056. In Canada: Elderhostel Canada, Corbett House, 29 Prince Arthur Ave., Toronto, Canada M5R 1B2.

INTERHOSTEL

An international study-travel program for peppy people over the age of 50 (a companion may be 40), Interhostel is sponsored by the University of New Hampshire. It offers two-week programs at colleges and universities in over 20 countries in Europe, Asia, Central America, Africa, New Zealand, and Australia. The idea is to stay in one place long enough to learn a lot about it, rather than taking a whirlwind tour. So, if you go, you'll come back well acquainted with the country you're visiting. During your stay, you are introduced to its history, culture, and people through a combination of lectures, field trips, and social activities. Your group—limited to 40 people—will be accompanied by a representative of the University of New Hampshire, just to make sure all goes well. The trips are scheduled year-round.

Your living quarters—clean and comfortable, though not necessarily fancy—will be in residence halls or modest hotels. Most meals are served cafeteria-style and feature the local food of the region. The cost, which is moderate for what you get, includes two weeks' full room and board, tuition, and ground transportation.

Because Interhostel's adventures impose a rigorous schedule of activities and happenings, the agency looks for people who are healthy and fit, full of vim and vigor, and able to tote their own luggage and walk at a moderate pace for at least a mile or two.

Among the current enticements are two-week trips to England, the Scottish Highlands, Eastern Europe, Ireland, Germany, Portugal, Sweden, Switzerland, Spain, China, and more, all of which cost $1,300 to $1,800 plus airfare. Longer adventures to Australia, New Zealand, Thailand, and China cost a bit more.

For information: Interhostel, University of New Hampshire, 6 Garrison Ave., Durham, NH 03824; 1-800-733-9753 or 603-862-1147, 8 A.M. to 4:30 P.M. eastern time.

NORTHEASTERN SENIOR SEMINARS

If you're 55 or older, you are eligible to enroll in a series of inexpensive one-week summer residential "campus vacations" at several New York universities. You choose courses from a range of classes from economics to psychology to folk dancing, live in a dorm, and take part in activities on and off campus. There are also commuter and single rates. The schools offering the Senior Seminars are Skidmore College, Long Island University at Southampton, and Ithaca College.

For information: Summer Special Programs, Skidmore College, Saratoga Springs, NY 12866-1632; 518-584-5000.

UNIVERSITY VACATIONS (UNIVAC)

Open to students of all ages, including yours, Univac puts you up in a comfortable room for sessions of a week to 12 days in April, July, August, or September at Oxford or Cambridge in England, Trinity College in Ireland, or the Sorbonne in Paris. Here mornings are spent attending a series of lectures presented by university scholars, with each session concentrating on a specific subject such as Chaucer's England, Medieval Life, Great Castles and Cathedrals, and the England of Henry James and T. S. Eliot. Afternoons are free for excursions or explorations. Again, the costs aren't likely to break the bank.

For information: Oxford-Cambridge Univac, 9602 N.W. 13th St., Miami, FL 33172; 305-591-1736.

PEER LEARNING PROGRAMS

There are currently more than 40 learning programs within colleges and universities throughout the country whose basic concept is peer learning and teaching. This means that classes are led by members, rather than paid faculty, who have special expertise in the subject at hand. The study groups take the form of discussion seminars, lectures, workshops, studio classes, or field trips, with the curriculum planned by the members. In some cases, though not all, members must be retired professionals or executives.

There are no tests or grades, although there may be assigned reading or other preparation, and the plan always includes social activities. Students pay an annual membership fee and may take as many courses as they wish. They also receive student status at the university, giving them all of the usual campus privileges, including the use of the library and the swimming pool.

At many of the schools, you may also take one or two regular undergraduate courses each semester as part of your membership, either without charge or at reduced tuition.

Here is a sampling of peer learning programs:

THE INSTITUTE FOR RETIRED PROFESSIONALS

At the New School for Social Research in New York, established in 1962, this was the first such program. As the granddaddy of them all, it has served as a pilot program for similar schools at other institutions. It offers its members—about 650 retired professionals— more than 80 study groups in subjects ranging from Virginia Woolf to Highlights of Mathematics to Bridge for Beginners. Members may also enroll in one regular daytime New School course each semester.

For information: Institute for Retired Professionals, New School for Social Research, 66 W. 12th St., New York, NY 10011; 212-741-5682.

ACADEMY OF LIFELONG LEARNING

For information: University of Delaware, 2800 Pennsylvania Ave., CED, Wilmington, DE 19806; 302-573-4433.

CENTER FOR CREATIVE RETIREMENT
For information: Long Island University, Southampton, NY 11968-4198; 516-283-4000.

CENTER FOR LEARNING IN RETIREMENT
For information: University of California Extension Center, 55 Laguna St., San Francisco, CA 94102; 415-863-4518.

DONOVAN SCHOLARS PROGRAM
A study program at the University of Kentucky in Lexington and at the 14 UK community colleges in Kentucky, the Donovan Scholars Program was designed specifically for students over the age of 65. It provides free tuition in all undergraduate or graduate courses in all academic areas. In addition, there are special non-credit course offerings for those over 60 in such subjects as art, music appreciation, radio-drama, and exercise. Discussion groups meet twice a week and an annual week-long writing workshop (for people over 57) is held every summer.
For information: Donovan Scholars Program, Ligon House, University of Kentucky, Lexington, KY 40506-0442; 606-257-2656.

DUKE INSTITUTE FOR
LEARNING IN RETIREMENT
Here some of the classes are led by peers, while others are taught by university faculty and local professionals.
For information: Duke University, Durham, NC 27708; 919-684-6259.

NEVER-TOO-OLD-TO-LEARN DEPARTMENT

SeniorNet started out at the University of San Francisco as a research project to study the use of computer communication networking by people in the over-49 crowd. But it has developed into a club for learners and users of computers. Members may use the equipment at any of the almost 40 sites throughout the country or join the national on-line computer network via their own computers, modems, software, and phone lines at home.

As a member of SeniorNet, you can send electronic mail to other members; have access to electronic services, programs, and databases; participate in discussions on specific topics; and take part in on-line conferences with the rest of the membership. A manual tells you how to hook up to the network, and a monthly newsletter keeps you up on the latest developments. A membership directory provides information about the interests, expertise, and backgrounds of the rest of the group, allowing you to choose people you'd like to communicate with.

If you live near a SeniorNet site, usually at a college, you can go there for courses, networking, and sociability. There are about 30 centers at this writing, and more are in the works.

Annual membership costs $25 and includes the newsletter, the handbook, and a guide that tells you how to connect to the network and make use of its functions. You must pay for your own network time.

For information: SeniorNet, 399 Arguello Blvd., San Francisco, CA 94118; 415-750-5030.

THE HARVARD INSTITUTE FOR LEARNING IN RETIREMENT

For information: Harvard Institute for Learning in Retirement, Lehman Hall B-3, Cambridge, MA 02138; 617-495-4973.

THE INSTITUTE FOR
LEARNING IN RETIREMENT

For information: The American University, Nebraska Hall, 4400 Massachusetts Ave. NW, Washington, DC 20016; 202-885-3920.

INSTITUTE OF NEW DIMENSIONS

Palm Beach Junior College's peer learning school is held at three locations in Florida: Palm Beach Junior College Central Campus in Lake Worth; North Campus in Palm Beach Gardens; and Florida Atlantic University Center in West Palm Beach. Here the yearly fee is very low, and you may take an unlimited number of courses.

For information: Institute of New Dimensions, Palm Beach Junior College, 3160 PGA Blvd., Palm Beach Gardens, FL 33410; 305-622-2440, ext. 307.

NOVA COLLEGE INSTITUTE FOR
RETIRED PROFESSIONALS

For information: Nova College Institute for Retired Professionals, 3301 College Ave., Fort Lauderdale, FL 33314; 305-475-7036.

THE PLATO SOCIETY OF UCLA

For information: The Plato Society of UCLA, 10995 Le Conte Ave., Los Angeles, CA 90024; 213-825-7917.

PROFESSIONALS AND EXECUTIVES
IN RETIREMENT

For information: Hofstra University, 1000 Hempstead Turnpike, Hempstead, NY 11550; 516-560-6919.

**TEMPLE ASSOCIATION FOR
RETIRED PROFESSIONALS**
For information: Temple University, 1619 Walnut St.,
Philadelphia, PA 19103; 215-787-1505.

MORE GOOD WAYS
TO GET SMARTER

CHAUTAUQUA INSTITUTION

The "55 Plus" Weekends and the Residential Week for
Older Adults are sponsored by Chautauqua Institution.
For 115 years, people have been going to the shore of
Lake Chautauqua, 75 miles south of Buffalo, New York,
to a sort of cultural summer camp in a Victorian village.
The 856-acre hilltop compound offers a wide variety of
programs, including summer weeks and off-season
weekends especially for the over-55 crowd. These programs get filled up far in advance, so if you're interested, don't waste a moment.

The weekends each have a specific focus; for example,
the U.S. Constitution, natural history, world affairs, music and art, trade relations with Japan. They include
discussions, workshops, lectures, films, recreational activities, and evening entertainment and are led by professionals. Housing and meals are provided in a residence hall.

The Residential Weeks for Older Adults are similar
but longer and include lodging and meals as well as
admittance to other goings-on at the center. It's all quite
cheap—the current weekly cost of tuition, room, meals,
and planned activities for a week amounts to about $275
and for a weekend about $92.
For information: Helen Overs, Program Center of
Older Adults, Chautauqua, NY 14722; 716-357-6200.

CLOSE UP FOUNDATION

An "educational vacation" in Washington, DC, Close Up is designed for people who are at least 50. The idea is to give you a whole week of firsthand access to "inside" Washington. Activities include two or three seminars a day with key Washington personalities (senators, White House officials, foreign ambassadors, reporters, and others) on topics of current concern; daily briefings for background information; motorcoach tours of the city; a day on Capitol Hill; all meals, many at interesting restaurants; an evening at the theater; daily workshops to discuss issues and events; a banquet; and scheduled free time. You'll lodge in a good hotel.

All this, available to both groups and individuals, is quite inexpensive. That's because the weeks are offered in the spring and fall by the Close Up Foundation, a nonprofit, nonpartisan organization that has brought more than 310,000 people of all ages to Washington to study government "on location," in cooperation with the American Association of Retired Persons (AARP).

The Close Up Foundation also runs a Congressional Senior Citizen Intern Program, where you spend a week working in the office of your own senator or representative (for this program, sign up via his or her office). The qualifications: you must be 60, healthy, and willing to work.

For information: Close Up Foundation, 44 Canal Center Plaza, Alexandria, VA 22314; 1-800-232-2000 (in Virginia, 703-706-3672).

THE COLLEGE AT 60

Part of Fordham University and located at the Lincoln Center campus in New York City, the College at 60 offers credit courses in liberal arts subjects such as history, psychology, philosophy, economics, literature, music, art, and computers, taught by Fordham faculty members. Included are a lecture series and the use of all college facilities. After taking four seminars, students receive a certificate and are encouraged to enter the regular Fordham University program.

Believe it or not, you are eligible for the College at 60 when you are over 50.

For information: The College at 60, Fordham University at Lincoln Center, 113 W. 60th St., New York, NY 10023; 212-636-6740.

THE EDUCATIONAL NETWORK FOR OLDER ADULTS

This not-for-profit organization in Chicago, which charges nothing for its services, is a network of 65 colleges and universities, adult organizations, community centers, and associations. Its purpose is to help older people in the greater Chicago area find the educational and training programs they need.

ENOA's Resource Center will answer questions on anything "from getting a GED, vocational training and further academic education to finding a bridge group, getting a manuscript published, finding volunteer work, starting a new business, or locating financial-retirement planning seminars." In other words, it's there to help.

For information: The Education Network for Older Adults, 36 S. Wabash, Suite 624, Chicago, IL 60603; 312-782-8967.

THE NEW ENGLAND SENIOR ACADEMY

A weekend residential program, the New England Senior Academy is designed for older people with a love of learning. It is sponsored by the New England Center and the New England Land Grant Universities: University of Connecticut, University of Maine, University of Massachusetts/Amherst, University of New Hampshire, University of Rhode Island, and University of Vermont. The weekend sessions at the New England Center on the campus of the University of New Hampshire begin on Friday evening with a buffet dinner and end with Sunday brunch. Your time is spent in discussions, lectures and demonstrations as well as special events. Each weekend focuses on a specific subject—from art and literature to history and culture—with courses and discussions led by university faculty.

For information: New England Senior Academy, New England Center Program Office, 15 Stafford Ave., University of New Hampshire, Durham, NH 03824-3560; 603-862-1900.

THE NORTH CAROLINA CENTER FOR CREATIVE RETIREMENT

Designed to help the graying set forth on a fulfilling life when they no longer have to spend all their energies on their jobs, this is an unusual setup. For those over 50, it features eight components: a Pre-Retirement Institute to help people make wise decisions about when, where, and how to spend their retirement; the College for Seniors, with a range of courses within the University of North Carolina, including travel-study courses in many parts of the world; an institute that holds workshops on vital issues such as housing options and finances; a leadership program of accomplished people who provide their expertise to the community and the university; an educational health program; a service league; a council that provides consulting for small businesses; and a research institute. That's a big handful of programs put together for the first time under one umbrella.

For information: The North Carolina Center for Creative Retirement, University of North Carolina at Asheville, Asheville, NC 28804-3299; 704-251-6512.

OASIS

OASIS (Older Adult Service and Information System) is a nonprofit organization sponsored by the May Department Stores Company in collaboration with local hospitals, medical centers, government agencies, and other participants in 26 locations across the nation. Its purpose is to enrich the lives of people over 55 by providing educational, cultural, and wellness programs to its members. At its centers, OASIS offers classes ranging from French conversation and the visual arts to dance, bridge, creative writing, history, exercise, classical music, points of law, and prevention of osteoporosis. Also featured are special events such as concerts, plays, and museum exhibits; lectures; volunteer opportunities; and even trips and cruises. If you live in an OASIS city, sign up—this is a good deal. Membership is free.

For information: OASIS, 7710 Carondelet Ave., Ste. 125, St. Louis, MO 63105; 314-862-2933.

UNIVERSITY SENIORS

Membership in this New York University program for people over 65 gets you two university courses per semester and biweekly luncheon seminars on subjects of current interest, all for a moderate fee. Recent topics have included U.S. economic power, criminal behavior in America, and myths and the Bible.

For information: University Seniors, NYU School of Continuing Education, 11 W. 42nd St., New York, NY 10036; 212-790-1330.

GETTING AN EDUCATION IN CANADA

Virtually every college and university in Canada offers free tuition to students over the age of 60 or 65, whether they attend classes part-time or full-time. Colleges of applied arts and technology generally offer postsecondary credit courses through their Departments of Continuing Education or Extension to seniors and charge a mere $5 or $10 per course. Aside from the nonexistent or low cost, seniors are treated just like the other students, have the same privileges, and must abide by the same regulations.

For information: Write to the registrar of the college you've chosen for information about its program or, for general information, to the Ministry of Colleges and Universities in your province.

Chapter Seventeen
Shopping Breaks, Taxes, Insurance, and Other Practical Matters

This chapter is not filled with great suggestions for having fun, but the information here may tip you off to some facts you didn't know as well as benefits that are coming your way simply because you've lived so long!

SAVING MONEY IN THE STORES

Clever marketing experts have recently realized that the over-50s, a segment now growing three times faster than the rest of the country's population, is the next target market. We not only have more money to spend but are more inclined to spend it than younger consumers. On the other hand, we're a bunch of cautious consumers who know the value of a dollar and are always on the lookout for a bargain.

A couple of large national department store chains offer some special services and enticements to shoppers over 50.

SEARS ROEBUCK & CO.
Sears started Mature Outlook several years ago as an over-50 club. Along with the club's other benefits, it offers sizable retail price cuts at Sears stores, which members get by cashing in special discount coupons

good for a variety of products and services. The coupons come your way regularly once you've joined the organization and may be used in Sears stores in the United States and Canada. See Chapter 19 for the details on signing up with Mature Outlook.

MONTGOMERY WARD
Montgomery Ward's Y.E.S. (Years of Extra Savings) Discount Club, a very good deal indeed, saves you money in many ways when you've reached the magic age of 55. As a member, you receive a membership card and a bimonthly magazine. The membership fee is currently $2.90 per month for you and your spouse. With the membership card in hand, you will get 10 percent off any merchandise, sale or nonsale, in Montgomery Ward stores every Tuesday. On Tuesdays, Wednesdays, and Thursdays, you're entitled to 10 percent off any auto service charges. On Tuesdays, the 10 percent comes off auto parts as well. Any day, when you buy a gift you get a free gift box.

What's more, the Y.E.S. Club Travel Service plans your travel, makes reservations, and gives you good discounted prices *plus* cash rebates on the cost of your trips. This means that upon your return you will receive a check for a 10 percent rebate on all hotels/motels and car rentals, and 5 percent on tours and cruises.
For information: Montgomery Ward Y.E.S. Discount Club, 200 N. Martingale Rd., Schaumburg, IL 60173; 1-800-421-5396.

FEDERAL INCOME TAXES

The most recent tax law does not provide an extra exemption for those over 65 years of age. Instead, it gives you a larger standard deduction than younger people are entitled to, according to Julian Block, author of "The Homeowner's Tax Guide."

The standard deductions on the short non-itemized income-tax form for everyone *under* 65 for 1991 returns are $5,700 for married couples filing jointly, $2,850 each for married people filing separately, $3,400 for single people, and $5,000 for single heads of households. (These standard deductions change every year to reflect inflation, so be sure to check them out for each upcoming year's return.)

However, if one spouse of a couple filing jointly is *over* 65, the standard deduction is increased for 1991 returns (by $650) to $6,350. If both members of a married couple are over 65, it is increased (by $650 twice) to $7,000. For a married person over 65 filing separately, the deduction increases (by $650) to $3,500. A single person over 65 may deduct $4,250 ($850 more than those who are younger). And a head of household over 65 gets a standard deduction in 1991 of $5,850 ($850 more than an under-65).

None of this applies, of course, if you itemize your deductions.

By the way, the Internal Revenue Service issues a free booklet, "Tax Information for Older Americans" (Publication 554). Call 1-800-TAX-FORM or pick one up at your local IRS office.

SALE OF PRINCIPAL RESIDENCE

You can save money on taxes if you are (or your spouse is) 55 when you sell the home you have owned and lived in as a principal residence for at least three years out of the five-year period ending on the date of the sale. You may elect to exclude from your gross income for federal tax purposes up to $62,500 if you are married and filing separately or $125,000 if you are single or married and filing a joint return.

Before you decide to take advantage of this, however, be sure to discuss it with a tax consultant because this exclusion may be used only once in your lifetime and you may be better off saving the privilege for a later home sale.

A NEW LEASH ON LIFE

Through **Purina Pets for People**, an ingenious program funded by Ralston Purina, local humane organizations provide pets for people over 60 at no initial cost to the recipients. The program pays for adoption fees, initial veterinary visits, spaying or neutering, and a starter kit of pet supplies, and contributes a supply of Purina Dog Chow or Cat Chow pet food. The program is designed to rescue a passel of homeless pets, a lot of them grown and trained, and give them to people who'd like the company. Of course, prospective owners must pass their local shelter's screening procedure to be sure they can provide the proper care.

For information: Purina Pets for People, Checkerboard Sq., 6T, St. Louis, MO 63164.

GETTING HELP WITH YOUR TAX RETURN

Tax assistance is usually available to you free through the Internal Revenue Service or other private and public organizations. Check your telephone book for the appropriate addresses and telephone numbers. Or call your local tax department.

Better yet, contact the Tax-Aide service provided by American Association of Retired Persons (see Chapter 19) which now has thousands of sites around the country where volunteer tax counselors help low- and moderate-

income taxpayers over 60 to complete their forms. Watch
your local newspaper for the office nearest you or write
to Tax-Aide Section, AARP, 601 E St. NW, Washington,
DC 20049.

AUTO AND HOMEOWNER'S INSURANCE

Mature people tend to be good drivers, becoming a
much better risk class as a group than the younger
crowd. You tend to be more careful drivers, having shed
most of your hot-rod habits by now, and drive fewer
miles. Therefore, statistically, you have about 10 percent
fewer accidents per year than other risk categories do.
These are the reasons many insurance companies offer
discounts on your automobile coverage once you've
reached a certain age.

Some companies even offer reductions in premiums
for homeowner's insurance as well, figuring you have
become a more cautious and reliable sort who takes good
care of your property.

Although discounts are wonderful and we all love to
get them, they are not the whole picture, according to
consumer advocate Robert Hunter of The National Insurance Consumers Organization: "You should shop the
bottom line rather than discounts alone, always considering what you pay for the coverage you get. If a company
charges higher premiums than other companies for com-
parable coverage and then gives you a discount, you
haven't profited at all. Go for the bottom line with a
reputable company."

Because insurance regulations differ from state to
state, a complete list of companies giving discounts for

age is impossible to assemble. It is best to go through an insurance agent or your state's insurance department. The following, however, are some of the special offerings of major firms in many states.

AETNA

In most states, Aetna gives a discount of about 10 percent off the premium on liability and collision coverage to good drivers 55 to 64 and about 20 percent to those over 65. And, over 55, you also get approximately 40 percent off on comprehensive auto coverage (fire and theft). Driving must be for pleasure use only.

HOW TO SAVE YOUR LIFE

If you happen to have the misfortune of falling ill or having an accident while you're away from home, **MedicAlert** may save your health—or even your life. When you join this nonprofit foundation (lifetime membership costs $30), you receive a metal bracelet or neck chain engraved with your personal identification number and a 24-hour-a-day call-collect telephone number tied into a data bank in California. When you or medical personnel call the data bank, all of your backup medical information is provided along with names and telephone numbers of your physician, next of kin, people to notify in an emergency, and other relevant information. As a backup, you get a wallet card containing the same material.

If you want your bracelet or neck chain in gold or silver, membership will cost you more.

For information: To register by credit card, call 1-800-ID-ALERT. Or write to MedicAlert Foundation, PO Box 1009, Turlock, CA 95381.

ALLSTATE
Allstate gives a 10 percent discount across the board—for all coverage—on both auto and homeowner's policies to people who are at least 55 and retired.

CHUBB
Chubb's offer is 10 percent off for drivers over 50 on liability and collision coverage and a 20 percent discount on comprehensive. Cars must be used for pleasure only, and there may be no youthful drivers (under 25) in the household.

GEICO
Good drivers from ages 50 to 65, using their cars for pleasure only, are given a Prime Time Rating and a discounted premium. Over 65, you're back where you started, however. Homeowners over 50 and retired get a 10 percent discount.

COLONIAL PENN
This company gives a retirement discount if you use your car only for pleasure.

HARTFORD
The company that services American Association of Retired Persons (see Chapter 19) offers members of this organization a discount of about 10 percent for completing an accredited defensive-driving course and up to 10 percent for maintaining a safe driving record. There are also lifetime renewal agreements, credits for low annual mileage, and full 12-month policies.

On homeowner's insurance, Hartford/AARP offers 5 percent credit on your total premium at any age in most states if you are retired.

LIBERTY MUTUAL
Special discounted rates are given by Liberty Mutual across the board on automobile insurance for those over 65.

NATIONWIDE
Nationwide gives a discount of 10 percent on all automobile coverage for people 55 and over.

US F & G
This company offers a discount of approximately 10 percent on auto coverage for people over 65.

BANKING

Many banks offer special incentives and services to people over 55 or 60, ranging from free checking to free NOW accounts, elimination of savings-account fees, free insurance, travelers cheques, and safe-deposit boxes, and even cash rebates at restaurants. Every bank and every state is different, so you must check out the situation in your community. Do some careful comparison shopping to make sure you are getting the best deal available.

LEGAL ASSISTANCE

Call upon your local area senior agency, which is required by law to provide some legal assistance to older citizens. Yours may help you untangle some puzzling legal problems or, at least, tell you what services are available to you. Or contact the local bar association for information. It is quite possible that it operates a referral or pro bono program. Or, suggests the American Bar Association, ask your local Legal Services Program for help or referrals.

Chapter Eighteen

Volunteer for
Great Experiences

There's no need to hang around letting your talents and abilities go to waste once you've quit working for a living. If, perhaps for the first time in your life, you now have hours to spare, maybe you'd like to spend some of them volunteering your services to good causes. There is plenty of work waiting for you. You can find it on your own, of course, but it may be simpler to use the resources of the many programs that are designed specifically to take advantage of your wisdom and experience.

But, first, keep in mind:

Remember, when you file your federal income tax, you are allowed to deduct unreimbursed expenses incurred while volunteering your services. These include transportation, parking, tolls, meals and lodging (in some cases), and uniforms.

The following programs and organizations are actively looking for you and will make a match between you and those who need your help.

RETIRED SENIOR VOLUNTEER PROGRAM
Part of the government's national volunteer agency AC-TION, RSVP serves as a referral and placement service,

matching people over 60 with appropriate volunteer work. Operating through local nonprofit private organizations or public agencies, RSVP is tailor-made for each community. In other words, whatever needs doing in your neighborhood is what you'll have a chance to do. You may choose hotlines; provide counseling on drug abuse, nutrition, finances, taxes, home repairs, or wills; or work in crime prevention, home care, or support groups.

For information: Contact your local or regional RSVP or ACTION office or ACTION, 806 Connecticut Ave. NW, Washington, DC 20525; 202-634-9355.

THE SERVICE CORPS OF RETIRED EXECUTIVES

SCORE—which now includes ACE (Active Corps of Executives)—is a national organization of both active and retired professionals and business executives who offer their expertise free of charge to small businesses. SCORE counselors, who include lawyers, business executives, accountants, engineers, managers, journalists, and other specialists, provide management assistance and advice to small-business people who are going into business or who are already in business but need expert help.

With a current membership of more than 12,000 men and women, SCORE has about 400 chapters all over the mainland United States as well as Puerto Rico, Guam, and the Virgin Islands. Funded and coordinated by the government's Small Business Administration, it is operated and administered by its own elected officials.

For information: Contact your local U.S. Small Business Administration office or SCORE, 1129 20th St. NW, Suite 410, Washington, DC 20036; 202-653-6279.

KNITTERS, STITCHERS, AND CARVERS, UNITE!

Elder Craftsmen encourages and advises people over 55 who want to make and sell their own handcrafts. A nonprofit organization operating for more than 30 years, it runs a retail shop in New York that sells most handwork on consignment, with 60 percent of the price going to the artist. Sometimes, however, it provides patterns and materials to skilled workers who work at home to produce specific items in quantity, in which case the craftspeople are paid by the piece. It also offers training courses for representatives of agencies and community groups and serves as an advisory group when needed.
For information: The Elder Craftsmen, Inc., 135 E. 65th St., New York, NY 10021; 212-861-5260.

AARP VOLUNTEER TALENT BANK

This public service was organized by AARP, the vast over-50 club (see Chapter 19), to help those who wish to serve others. Says a spokesperson, "People over 50 have a lifetime of experience and skills which can apply to a variety of volunteer interests," and the Talent Bank puts people and work together. After you complete a questionnaire about your personal background, interests, and skills, the information is matched by computer with opportunities for volunteer work within American Association of Retired Persons or by referral to other organizations in your own community.
For information: AARP, 601 E St. NW, Washington, DC 20049; 202-434-AARP.

PEACE CORPS

No doubt you've always thought the Peace Corps was reserved for young idealists right out of college. The truth is that it's a viable choice for idealists of any age.

There is no upper age limit for acceptance into the Peace Corps, and since its beginning in 1961 thousands of Senior Volunteers have brought their talents and experience to developing countries in Latin America, the Caribbean, Africa, Asia, and the Pacific. To become a Senior Volunteer, you must be a U.S. citizen and meet basic legal and medical criteria. Some assignments require a college or technical-school degree or an experience equivalent. Married couples are eligible and will be assigned together.

What you get in return is the chance to travel, an unforgettable living experience in a foreign land, basic expenses, and housing, plus technical, language, and cultural training. And you will have a chance to use your expertise constructively in fields such as agriculture, engineering, math/science, home economics, education, skilled trades, forestry and fisheries, and community development.

For information: Peace Corps, Room P-301, Washington DC 20526; 1-800-424-8580, ext. 93.

ENVIRONMENTAL PROTECTION AGENCY, SEE PROGRAM

The Senior Environmental Employment (SEE) Program, an EPA-funded project, employs people over 55 part-time or full-time in jobs that help fight environmental pollution. If you sign up, you will be paid an hourly fee not much higher than minimum wage, but, on the other hand, you'll be helping to clean up America.

For information: Contact your regional EPA office or send a letter and résumé to Senior Environmental Employment Program, EPA, 401 M St. SW, Washington, DC 20460.

VOLUNTEERS IN TECHNICAL ASSISTANCE

VITA provides another avenue for helping developing countries. A nonprofit international organization, VITA provides volunteer experts who respond—usually by direct correspondence—to technical inquiries from people in these nations who need assistance in such areas as small-business development, energy applications, agriculture, reforestation, water supply and sanitation, and low-cost housing. Its volunteers also perform other services such as project planning, translations, publications, marketing strategies, evaluations, and technical reports and often become on-site consultants.

There is no minimum age, but you must be retired to serve. If you become a volunteer, you will not be paid, but will be reimbursed for your travel and living expenses.

For information: Volunteers in Technical Assistance, 1815 N. Lynn St., Suite 200, Arlington, VA 22209; 703-276-1800.

FOSTER GRANDPARENTS PROGRAM

This federal program sponsored by the government's national volunteer agency ACTION offers gratifying volunteer work to thousands of low-income men and women 60 and over, in communities all over the 50 states, Puerto Rico, Virgin Islands, and the District of Columbia. The volunteers, who receive 40 hours of preservice orientation and training and four hours a month of inservice training, work with children who have special needs—boarder babies; troubled children; handicapped, severely retarded, abandoned, delinquent, abused, hospitalized, addicted, forlorn children who are desperate for love, care, and attention and do not get it from their families. They may work in hospitals, schools, homes, day-care programs, or residential centers.

Volunteers, who must be in good health although they may be handicapped, work 20 hours a week. For this, they receive, aside from the immense satisfaction, a small tax-free annual stipend, a transportation allowance, hot meals while at work, accident and liability insurance, and annual physicals.

For information: Contact your local senior agency or Foster Grandparents Program, ACTION, 806 Connecticut Ave. NW, Washington, DC 20525; 202-634-9355.

FOR JOB HUNTERS

If you're over 45 and in the market for a job but don't know where to start looking for one, hook up with Operation ABLE, a nonprofit organization affiliated with agencies that will help match you with a likely employer. You're in luck if you live in Chicago, where there are five regional offices. In addition, there is a network of independent ABLE-like organizations, modeled after the original, in several other cities, including New York; Boston; Detroit; Los Angeles; San Francisco; Little Rock, Arkansas; Brattleboro, Vermont; and Lincoln, Nebraska.

Operation ABLE tries every which way to get you into the working world. It provides job counseling, on-the-job training, group training activities, and individual career assessment and guidance; teaches job-hunting skills; matches older workers with employers; operates a pool of temporaries; and offers myriad other services.

For information: Operation ABLE, 180 N. Wabash Ave., Chicago, IL 60601.

FORTY PLUS CLUBS

Offices in 16 cities throughout the United States comprise this nonprofit cooperative of unemployed executives, managers, and professionals, men and women, 40 years of age or more. Their objective is to help members conduct effective job searches and find new jobs. There is no paid staff. The members do all the work and help pay expenses with their one-time charge of from $350 to $850, depending on location (paid in installments), plus moderate dues. They must commit themselves to attend weekly meetings and spend at least two days a week working at the club and assisting others in their search for work.

In return, members are helped to examine their career skills and define their goals, counseled on résumé writing and interview skills, helped to plan marketing strategy, and given job leads. They may also use the club as a base of operations, with phone answering and mail service, computers, reference library.

Forty Plus Clubs exist at this writing in New York City and Buffalo, New York; Oakland and Los Angeles (with a branch in Laguna Hills), California; Denver (with subsidiaries in Fort Collins and Colorado Springs), Colorado; Chicago, Illinois; Columbus, Ohio; Dallas and Houston, Texas; Salt Lake City, Utah; Philadelphia, Pennsylvania; Seattle, Washington; Washington, DC; and Honolulu, Hawaii.

For information: Addresses of the clubs and descriptive material are available from Forty Plus of New York, 15 Park Row, New York, NY 10038; 212-233-6086.

INTERNATIONAL EXECUTIVE SERVICE CORPS

IESC, organized and directed by U.S. business executives, is a nonprofit organization that recruits retired highly skilled executives and technical advisors to assist businesses in the developing nations. It is funded by the U.S. Agency for International Development (AID), overseas clients and foreign governments, and many American corporations.

After being briefed on the country and the client, volunteer executives travel overseas—with their spouses, if they wish—for projects that generally last two to three months. IESC pays for the couple's travel expenses and provides a per diem allowance.

For information: International Executive Service Corps, PO Box 10005, Stamford, CT 06904; 203-967-6000.

NATIONAL EXECUTIVE SERVICE CORPS

This nonprofit organization performs a unique service: it helps other nonprofit organizations solve their problems by providing retired executives with extensive corporate and professional experience to serve as volunteer consultants. Its services are offered in five basic areas—education, health, the arts, social services, and religion—and the assistance covers everything from organizational structure and financial systems to marketing and funding strategy. Volunteers' expenses are covered.

For information: National Executive Service Corps, 257 Park Ave. South, New York, NY 10010; 212-529-6660.

NATIONAL PARK SERVICE

If you love the outdoors and have the time, volunteer to work for the National Park Service as a VIP (Volunteers in Parks). VIPs are not limited to over-50s, but a good portion of them are retired people with time, expertise, talent, and interest in forests and wilderness. You may work a few hours a week or a month, seasonally or full-time, and may or may not—depending on the park—wear a uniform or get reimbursed for out-of-pocket expenses. The job possibilities range from working at an information desk to serving as a guide, maintaining trails, driving a shuttle bus, painting fences, designing computer programs, patrolling trails, making wildlife counts, writing visitor brochures, and preparing park events.

For information: Contact the VIP coordinator at the national park where you would like to volunteer and request an application. Or, for addresses, contact the appropriate National Park Service regional office.

VOLUNTEER PROGRAMS IN ISRAEL

VOLUNTEERS FOR ISRAEL

In this volunteer work-and-cultural program for adults 18 to 70 in Israel you'll put in eight-hour days for three weeks, sleep in a segregated dormitory, and work in small groups at a reserve or supply military base, doing whatever needs doing most at that moment. You may serve in supply, warehousing, or maintenance of equipment or in social services in hospitals. You'll wear an army uniform with a "Civilian Volunteer" patch. Board, room, and other expenses are free, but you must pay for your own subsidized airfare.

For information: Volunteers for Israel, 330 West 42nd St., New York, NY 10036-6902; 212-643-4848.

ACTIVE RETIREES IN ISRAEL (ARI)
Sponsored by B'nai B'rith International, ARI is a volunteer work program for people who are 50, in good health, and members of B'nai B'rith. Volunteers pay for the opportunity to live in the resort city of Netanya and work in the mornings for two-and-a-half winter months in hospitals, forests, kibbutzim, schools, and facilities for the elderly and the handicapped. Afternoons are spent learning Hebrew, while the evenings include concerts, discussion groups, and cultural activities. Guided tours of the country are part of the program.

For information: ARI, B'nai B'rith Israel Commission, 1640 Rhode Island Ave. NW, Washington, DC 20036; 202-857-6580.

JNF ISRAEL WORK STUDY PROGRAM
In this program sponsored by the Jewish National Fund, you'll spend two or three months in Israel working five mornings a week. You'll also study Hebrew, tour the small desert country, and learn the culture. You must be over 50 and in good enough shape to work hard. You'll have a choice of jobs—some volunteers choose to work in the forests, some in the schools, hospitals, homes for the aged, at army bases, universities, kibbutzim, or perhaps with local craftspeople or archaeologists. Afternoons are devoted to planned activities and evenings to socializing. Included are five days of touring and a month off in Jerusalem. The cost is all-inclusive.

For information: JNF Israel Work-Study Program, Migvan Events, 42 E. 69th St., New York, NY 10021; 212-879-9300.

Chapter Nineteen

The Over-50 Organizations and What They Can Do for You

W hen you consider that there are more people in this country over the age of 55 than there are children in elementary and high schools, you can see why we have powerful potential to influence what goes on around here. As the "demographic discovery of the decade," a group that controls most of the nation's disposable income, we've become an enormous marketing target. And, just like any other group of people, we've got plenty of needs.

A number of organizations in the United States and Canada have been formed in the last few years to act as advocates for the over-50 crowd and to offer us special deals and services. Here is a brief rundown on them and what they have to offer you. You may want to join more than one of them so you can reap the benefits of each.

THE AMERICAN ASSOCIATION OF RETIRED PERSONS

The biggest, oldest, and best known of all such organizations is AARP, a huge club with a vast array of services and programs. With about 33 million members (8,000 join every day), AARP is open to anyone anywhere in the world who's over 50, retired or not, and so it wields amazing power in the marketplace and among the nation's policy makers. Its bimonthly magazine, *Modern Maturity,* goes to more people than any other magazine in the country.

For a yearly membership fee of $5 (and that includes a spouse), AARP offers so many things that you are likely to stop reading before you get to the end of the list. But here are some of them:

- Supplemental health insurance at group rates provided by Prudential. All members are guaranteed eligibility.
- A nonprofit, mail-order pharmacy service that delivers by mail.
- Discounts at hotels, motels, and resorts and on auto rentals from Avis, Thrifty, Hertz, and National rental agencies.
- A travel service that offers preplanned tours, cruises, special-event programs and hosted living abroad, designed especially for mature voyagers (see Chapter 5).
- A motor club that gets you emergency road and towing service, trip planning, and other benefits.
- Auto and homeowner's insurance, via the Hartford Insurance Group, tailored for people over 50.
- ▶ *Modern Maturity* magazine, a bimonthly, full of general articles and useful information, plus a monthly news bulletin.
- ▶ A national advocacy and lobbying program to develop legislative objectives and priorities and represent the interests of older people at all levels of government, plus volunteer legislative committees that are active in every state.
- More than 4,000 local chapters with a range of activities and volunteer projects, from teaching to helping out at the polls.
- Volunteer-staffed programs such as tax-preparation assistance, driver retraining, widowed-persons counseling, and Medicare assistance.

▶ Special service programs in such areas as consumer affairs, legal counseling, tax information, housing and health advocacy, women's activities, and crime reduction.
▶ The Institute of Lifetime Learning, a national clearinghouse for educational programs for mature people (see Chapter 16).
▶ Free publications on a large number of subjects relevant to your life.
▶ And even more.

For information: AARP, 601 E St. NW, Washington, DC 20049; 202-434-AARP.

CANADIAN ASSOCIATION OF RETIRED PERSONS

For a few dollars a year you and your spouse can join CARP, a nonprofit association for Canadians over 50 (who make up almost a quarter of the country's population). Inspired by AARP, it provides you with discount rates on lots of good things, from health insurance to car rentals, hotels, theaters, and travel. It also sends you a quarterly newspaper called *CARP News*.

For information: CARP, 27 Queen St. East, Suite 304, Toronto, ON M5C 2M6, Canada; 416-363-8748.

CATHOLIC GOLDEN AGE

A Catholic nonprofit organization that is concerned with issues affecting older citizens, such as health care costs, housing, and social security benefits, the CGA has well over a million members and more than 200 chapters throughout the country. It offers many good things to its members who must be over 50. These include spiritual benefits such as masses and prayers throughout the world and practical benefits as well. Among them are discounts on hotels, motels, and campground sites, car rentals, prescriptions, eyeglasses. Other benefits include group insurance plans, pilgrimage and group travel programs, and an automobile club. Membership costs $7 a year.

For information: Catholic Golden Age, 400 Lackawanna Ave., Scranton, PA 18503; 1-800-233-4697.

NATIONAL COUNCIL OF SENIOR CITIZENS

An advocacy organization, NCSC lobbies on the local, state, and national level for legislation benefiting older Americans. With about 4.5 million members, it has carried on many successful campaigns in the areas of housing, health care, Social Security, and the like.

Although NCSC's major focus is its legislative program, it also has a local club network, social events, prescription discounts, group rates on supplemental health insurance, automobile insurance, and travel discounts, plus a newspaper that keeps you up to date on all of the above.

For information: National Council of Senior Citizens, 925 15th St. NW, Washington, DC 20005; 202-347-8800.

NATIONAL ASSOCIATION FOR RETIRED CREDIT UNION PEOPLE

Obviously, not everybody can join this club, but those who will get some good benefits. These include an attractive and useful magazine called *Prime Times* and the *NARCUP Newsletter*, car-rental discounts, Medicare-supplement insurance, pharmacy discounts, lodging discounts at some hotels and campgrounds, and a

motor club. Also, discounted travel packages and tours.
For information: NARCUP, PO Box 391, Madison, WI
53701; 608-238-4286.

NATIONAL ASSOCIATION OF RETIRED FEDERAL EMPLOYEES

As you have probably gathered, this is an association of
federal retirees and families. Its primary mission is to
protect the earned benefits of retired federal employees
via its lobbying program in Washington.
For information: NARFE, 1533 New Hampshire Ave.
NW, Washington, DC 20036; 202-234-0832.

OLDER WOMEN'S LEAGUE

The league is an advocacy group that works to improve
the lot of older women in this country—not an easy job.
Through a national organization and local chapters, it
provides educational materials, training for citizen advocates, informational publications and the like, dealing
with the important issues facing women as they grow
older.
For information: Older Women's League, 730 11th St.
NW, Suite 300, Washington, DC 20001; 202-783-6686.

NATIONAL ALLIANCE OF SENIOR CITIZENS

This national lobbying organization with more than two
million members has a decidedly conservative tilt-to-the-
right bias, so people with middle-of-the-road or liberal
views would not feel too much at home here. It works to
influence national policy "on key issues of great impor-
tance to America and her future." As a member you
receive newsletters and benefits that include group insurance, prescription discounts, discounts on car rentals,

lodgings, moving expenses, and an automobile club.
For information: National Alliance of Senior Citizens, 2525 Wilson Blvd., Arlington, VA 22201; 703-528-4380.

GRAY PANTHERS

With about 40,000 members of all ages, the Gray Panthers fight ageism and speak up for older Americans, reminding people "that people over 65 will not be pushed around by the Administration, not by callous landlords, not by nursing home profiteers, and not by an indifferent health care system. . . . Yet citizens past 65 are consistently the largest and most active voting block in the United States." Major areas of concern include social security, housing, nursing homes, Medicare, attitudes.
For information: Gray Panthers, 1424 16th St. NW, Ste. 602, Washington, DC 20036; 202-387-3111.

THE RETIRED OFFICERS ASSOCIATION

This group is open to anyone who has been a commissioned or warrant officer in the seven U.S. uniformed services. These folks receive lobbying representation on Capitol Hill and a magazine with articles devoted to matters of special interest to them. They may also take advantage of several benefits, including discounts on car rentals and motel lodgings, a travel program with "military fares" to many overseas destinations, sports tournaments, a mail-order prescription program, group health and life insurance plans, and a car lease-purchase plan. TROA also has many autonomous local chapters with their own activities and membership fees.
For information: The Retired Officers Association, 201 N. Washington St., Alexandria, VA 22314-2529; 703-549-2311.

Index